Get ready for...

Edexcel GCSE
English

Consultant: Tony Farrell

David Grant

Esther Menon

Alan Pearce

A PEARSON COMPANY

Published by Pearson Education Limited, a company incorporated in England and Wales, having its registered office at Edinburgh Gate, Harlow, Essex, CM20 2JE. Registered company number: 872828

www.pearsonschoolsandfecolleges.co.uk

Edexcel is a registered trademark of Edexcel Limited

Text © Pearson Education Limited 2011

First published 2011

15 14 13 12 11
10 9 8 7 6 5 4 3 2 1

British Library Cataloguing in Publication Data
A catalogue record for this book is available from the British Library.

ISBN 978 0 435047 45 0

Edited by Julia Naughton
Designed by Wooden Ark
Produced by Kamae Design, Oxford
Original illustrations © Pearson Education Limited 2011
Illustrated by John Hallett
Cover design by Wooden Ark
Cover photo © magicoven/Shutterstock

Printed and bound in the UK by Scotprint

Acknowledgements

The publisher would like to thank the following for their kind permission to reproduce their photographs:

(Key: b-bottom; c-centre; l-left; r-right; t-top)

6 Shutterstock.com: Alperium. **8 Rex Features:** Garo / Phanie. **10 Rex Features:** David Fisher. **16 Rex Features**. **18 Fotolia.com:** Elenathewise (l). **Pearson Education Ltd:** Gareth Boden (r). **24 Rex Features:** Steve Meddle. **26 Alamy Images:** Ingram Publishing. **30 Rex Features:** Liz Finlayson / Eddie Mitchell (l). **30-31 Getty Images:** Rubberball / Nicole Hill. **32 Getty Images:** Rubberball / Nicole Hill. **33 Alamy Images:** North Wind Picture Archives (r). **Stockdisc:** (l). **36 Getty Images:** Science & Society Picture Library. **38 Shutterstock.com:** Chungking. **39 Alamy Images:** Keith Morris. **40 Alamy Images:** David Robertson. **42 Rex Features:** Liz Finlayson / Eddie Mitchell (l). **43 Kobal Collection Ltd:** Columbia / Marvel. **44 Alamy Images:** StockImages (t). **Imagestate Media:** John Foxx Collection (b). **48 iStockphoto:** Cathy Britcliffe. **50 Rex Features:** NILS JORGENSEN. **52 Getty Images:** Bruno Barbier / Robert Harding. **54 Alamy Images:** Aaron Foster. **55 Alamy Images:** Photos 12 (b); B.A.E. Inc (t). **56 Alamy Images:** Peter Jordan_NE. **58 Alamy Images:** StockImages (b); David Robertson (tl). **Rex Features:** Liz Finlayson / Eddie Mitchell (tr). **59 Getty Images:** Bruno Barbier / Robert Harding (r). **iStockphoto:** Cathy Britcliffe (l). **62 Getty Images:** Keith Brofsky (l). **Pearson Education Ltd:** Studio 8 (r). **63 Rex Features:** Ken McKay. **64 Alamy Images:** Paul Doyle. **65 Pearson Education Ltd:** Studio 8. **67 Getty Images:** Keith Brofsky. **68 Pearson Education Ltd:** Lord and Leverett. **71 Rex Features:** Ken McKay / ITV. **73 Shutterstock.com:** Valukin Sergey. **74 Science Photo Library Ltd:** Library of Congress, Geography and Map Division. **75 Getty Images:** Image Source. **76 Alamy Images:** Angela Hampton Picture Library. **77 Rex Features:** Ken McKay. **81 Alamy Images:** Golden Pixels LLC. **84 Photolibrary.com:** Bob Watkins. **86 Rex Features:** ITV. **87 Alamy Images:** By Ian Miles-Flashpoint Pictures. **88 Image courtesy of The Advertising Archives**. **94 iStockphoto:** adrian beesley. **95 Alamy Images:** Tony Watson. **96 iStockphoto:** adrian beesley. **99 Scottish Viewpoint:** Gary Mcharg. **100 Alamy Images:** Lebrecht Music and Arts Photo Library. **101 Shutterstock.com:** Stuart Elflett. **102 Shutterstock.com:** Jane Rix. **103 Shutterstock.com:** Stuart Elflett. **104 iStockphoto:** Aleksandar Vrzalski. **104-105 Scottish Viewpoint:** Gary Mcharg. **106 Getty Images:** Kim Westerskov. **109 Alamy Images:** Paul Doyle. **114 Photodisc/C Squared Studios**. **116 Alamy Images:** mediablitzimages (uk) Limited (r). **Corbis:** moodboard (l). **118 Fotolia.com:** FikMik. **120 Shutterstock.com:** Jozef Sedmak (b); Cre8tive images (t). **121 Alamy Images:** National Geographic Image Collection (t). **122 Alamy Images:** Tony Watson. **125 Getty Images:** Rachele Totaro - www.flickr.com / roseinthedark.

All other images © Pearson Education

Every effort has been made to trace the copyright holders and we apologise in advance for any unintentional omissions. We would be pleased to insert the appropriate acknowledgement in any subsequent edition of this publication.
The authors and publisher would like to thank the following individuals and organisations for permission to reproduce copyright material:

pp.viii, 2: screenshot of Second Life website (www.secondlife.com) © Linden Research,
Inc; pp.viii, 1, 4 It's a Moma Propaganda for Maximedia poster "YouTube" is used by kind permission of Moma Propaganda; pp.1, 12 homepage screenshot of http://www.moshimonsters.com is used by kind permission of Mind Candy Limited; p.5 YouTube company history text from http://www.youtube.com/t/company_history is used by kind permission of YouTube; p.6 blog 'Cityville: Help choose which building(s) will be released next!' By Brandy Shaul. 14 December 2010 is used by permission of XXX; p.8 article 'Facebook users will be forced to change their names to escape cyber past' from http://www.dailymail.co.uk/sciencetech/article-1304004/Google-says-Facebook-users-change-names-escape-cyberpast.html. 18 August 2010. Is used by permission of the Daily Mail and Solo Syndication; p.10 article 'Rage Against The Machine sells half a million copies to pip Joe McElderry (and Simon Cowell) to the Christmas No.1 spot' from http://www.dailymail.co.uk/tvshowbiz/article-1237332/Rage-Against-The-Machine-beat-Joe-McElderry-claim-Christmas-number-one.html. 21 December 2009 is used by permission of the Daily Mail and Solo Syndication; p.16 article 'Janet Street-Porter: Why I hate Facebook' from http://www.dailymail.co.uk/news/article-1138445/Janet-Street-Porter-Why-I-hate-Facebook.html. 6 February 2009 is used by permission of the Daily Mail and Solo Syndication; p.22 sentence from Think you Know website is used by kind permission of the Think You Know team; p.32 article 'The real-life Sleeping Beauty' from http://www.dailymail.co.uk/news/article-1249895/Louisa-Ball-Real-life-Sleeping-Beauty-sleeps-weeks-time.html#ixzz17XF1VL92. 11 February 2010 is used by permission of the Daily Mail and Solo Syndication; p.32 article 'My kids are lazy little slobs – why DO I let them get away with it?' from http://www.dailymail.co.uk/femail/article-1231011/My-kids-lazy-little-slobs--DO-I-let-away-it.html. 26 November 2009 is used by permission of the Daily Mail and Solo Syndication; p.32 article 'Giving teenage pupils a lie in can boost their exam results' from http://www.dailymail.co.uk/news/article-1259589/Giving-teenage-pupils-lie-boost-exams-results.html. 22 March 2010 is used by permission of the Daily Mail and Solo Syndication; p.34 stills from Being Human © Touchpaper Television; p.39 "Experiment" Dictionary.com Unabridged. Random House, Inc. 20 December 2010. <Dictionary.com http://dictionary.reference.com/browse/experiment>; p.39 "Stunt" Collins English Dictionary - Complete & Unabridged 10th Edition. HarperCollins Publishers. 20 December 2010. <Dictionary.com http://dictionary.reference.com/browse/stunt>; p.40 article 'The real RAM raider: Angry sheep smashes up house after charging his own reflection and smashing through patio doors' from http://www.dailymail.co.uk/news/article-1312188/Rampaging-ram-smashes-house-crashing-patiodoors.html?ITO=1490. 16 September 2010. Is used by permission of the Daily Mail and Solo Syndication; p.42 article 'Vacuum Cleaner-Man! Inventor uses suction to crawl up a wall, Spider-Man-style' from http://www.dailymail.co.uk/sciencetech/article-1251157/So-long-suckers-Human-fly-scales-wall-using-vacuum-cleanersbought-Tesco.html. 16 February 2010 is used by permission of the Daily Mail and Solo Syndication; p.44 article 'Google Streetview mystery of man wearing horse's head' from http://www.mirror.co.uk/news/top-stories/2010/06/25/mystery-of-a-boy-called-horse-115875-22358392/. 25 June 2010. Is used by permission of the Mirror; p.44 article 'Girl, 15, tells of terror after being stalked through forest by a big cat she claims was a PANTHER' from http://www.dailymail.co.uk/news/article-1279834/Panther-stalked-schoolgirl-Forest-Dean.html. 21May 2010 is used by permission of the Daily Mail and Solo Syndication; p.48 article 'Inverary Castle Phantom' from http://www.forteantimes.com/strangedays/ghostwatch/4171/inverary_castle_phantom_harper.html. August 2010. Is used by permission of the Fortean Times and Dennis Publishing Ltd; p.50 advert for 'CRITTER CRUISER HAMSTER EXERCISE WHEEL' from http://www.the-rabbithutch-shop.com/critter-cruiser-hamster-exercise-ball-scalextric-ip861361.html; p.50 advert for 'paw power' at http://www.firebox.com/product/2204/Hamster-Racer-Set is used by permission of Firebox.com; pp.52–53 article 'All fall down' from http://www.forteantimes.com/features/articles/4237/all_fall_down.html. August 2010. Is used by permission of the Fortean Times and Dennis Publishing Ltd; p.56 article 'School stops ball games after noise complaints from neighbours' By Richard Harris. 18 September 2010. Used by permission of York Press; p.68 poem extract from Gerrit Darn Ya by Jean Mason found in the Black Country Bugle; p.96 Illuminations by Tony Harrison taken from Collected Poems published by Penguin Books is used by permission of Gordon Dickenson; p.99 Old Tongue by Jackie Kay taken from 'Darling: New and Selected Poems'. Bloodaxe Books, 2007. Used by permission; pp.104, 106 Sea Fever by John Masefield is used by permission of the Society of Authors as the Literary Representative of the Estate of John Masefield; p.105 Geography Lesson by Brian Patten taken from 'Juggling with Gerbils', published by Puffin Books 2000; p.109 White Comedy by Benjamin Zephaniah taken from 'Propa Propaganda. Bloodaxe Books, 1996. Used by permission; p.111Life for Us by Choman Hardi taken from 'Life for Us'. Bloodaxe Books, 2004. Used by permission; p.116 article: experience – I threw £100,000 in the bin by Emal Celikkanat. 22 May 2010. Is used by permission of the Guardian; p.116 article: experience – I served 25 years for a crime I didn't commit by Robert Brown. 2 May 2009. Is used by permission of the Guardian; p.118 extract from The Passage by Justin Cronin, published by Orion Books on 24 June 2010 and is used by permission of Orion Books; p.119 extract from: The Vows of Silence by Susan Hill, published by Chatto & Windus. Used by permission of The Random House Group Ltd; p.122 The Boy Outside the Fire Station by Simon Armitage. Taken from 'Zoom!'. Bloodaxe Books, 2002. Used by permission; p.124 images © The Blue Cross.

Every effort has been made to contact copyright holders of material reproduced in this book. Any omissions will be rectified in subsequent printings if notice is given to the publishers.

Disclaimer
This material has been published on behalf of Edexcel and offers high-quality support for the delivery of Edexcel qualifications.

This does not mean that the material is essential to achieve any Edexcel qualification, nor does it mean that it is the only suitable material available to support any Edexcel qualification. Edexcel material will not be used verbatim in setting any Edexcel examination or assessment. Any resource lists produced by Edexcel shall include this and other appropriate resources.

Copies of official specifications for all Edexcel qualifications may be found on the Edexcel website: www.edexcel.com

Contents

Introduction for students

This book is designed to be fun preparation for the GCSE study that you will eventually move onto. By focusing on the kinds of skills you will need when you start GCSE, it gives you a head start with your English studies. It is broken down into four units:

Unit 1 The Digital World

In this unit you get the chance to study texts from or about the digital world, including Facebook, YouTube and virtual worlds.

Unit 1 will help you develop your reading and writing skills in relation to media and non-fiction texts. These are very useful skills to have: when you come to tackling GCSE English, you will eventually complete a **controlled assessment** in which you will answer questions on a number of media and non-fiction texts as well as writing one of your own texts. By learning these skills now you're giving yourself a head start.

Unit 2 Strange But True

The world of news and media can be weird and wonderful, and in this unit you'll see just how weird it can get. From the human spiderman to hamster mobiles to 'horse boy' – it's all in here.

Like Unit 1, Unit 2 helps you develop your reading and writing skills in relation to media and non-fiction texts, giving you the chance to practise and improve your responses.

Unit 3 The Language Of Teenagers

The way someone speaks – including what they say and how they say it – can reveal a lot about a person. In this unit you will look at your own spoken language and explore areas such as why it changes, what kind of first impression you might make and what your attitudes are to the ways in which other people talk.

Unit 3 will help you develop your spoken language analysis skills and your ability to write for the spoken voice. When you start GCSE, you will need to complete an analysis of a piece of spoken language as part of your controlled assessment and to write a text in the spoken voice, such as a speech. Unit 3 will help you get to grips with the basics of spoken language analysis.

What is controlled assessment?

This is one of the ways in which you will be assessed at GCSE (the other is through an exam). Controlled assessment basically means that you have a number of hours to prepare for and write your assessed piece of work. Any work is carried out under 'controlled conditions', which really means that it has to be completed in class under the supervision of a teacher.

Unit 4 Get Creative

Effective creative writing doesn't just happen by accident: there are a number of techniques and devices that writers can use to bring their texts to life. In this unit you get the chance to explore a range of poetry and also to attempt your own pieces of creative writing, including stories, articles and transcripts.

At GCSE you will need to analyse and write about poems, either in an exam or as controlled assessment. You will also need to write at least one piece of creative writing at GCSE. The skills developed in Unit 4 will help prepare you for these parts of GCSE.

How does the student book work?

This shows what you will be learning about in the lesson.

This shows how the lesson is relevant to what you will do when you start GCSE.

These features give you advice or warnings and are there to help you improve your work.

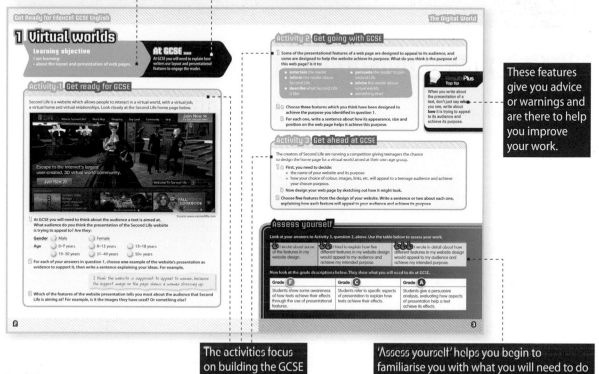

The activities focus on building the GCSE skills step-by-step.

'Assess yourself' helps you begin to familiarise you with what you will need to do to move up the grades when you start GCSE.

On these pages you get the chance to be the examiner and grade other students' work.

By working out which answer gets which grade, you will also understand what you need to do to improve your own work.

Introduction for teachers

The Get Ready resources are designed specifically to smooth the transition from KS3 to GCSE and to help your students achieve their potential by building GCSE skills in Year 9.

What are transitional resources?

The removal of SATs in 2009 has for many schools changed the function and purpose of Year 9. Where previously many weeks were spent preparing for the test, and where progress in KS3 was largely measured by SATs, this is no longer the case. Schools and departments have been left with the question of what to *do* with Year 9.

Teaching a full third year of the KS3 national curriculum can feel repetitive to students, who may also question the purpose of what they are doing: as much as SATs were disliked, they did prove a motivational tool for many teachers. Students could understand and be motivated by the idea of sitting a test, the outcome of which would capture their progress over the key stage. No longer.

The same students, however, may not be ready to start GCSE early – the demands and pressures of GCSE studies and assessments may prove too great for many Year 9 students. A neat solution, then, is the idea of transitional teaching: focusing on building GCSE skills but without actually starting on the GCSE course. This is exactly what these Get Ready materials set out to do.

Resources from Pearson

As well as this Student Book, Pearson has created other resources to support your planning and delivery.

- **Teacher Guide** – a bank of full colour visual lesson plans can be found in the corresponding Teacher Guide, written by experienced teachers, examiners and EAL experts. These lesson plans make use of and reference the BBC Active video footage and other resources on the ActiveTeach CD-ROM as well as providing support for EAL students, written by NALDIC. What's more, the Teacher Guide is accompanied by a CD-ROM containing all the lessons plans as Word files, so they are fully customisable.
- **ActiveTeach CD-ROM** – an onscreen version of the Student Book complete with a wealth of digital assets including exclusive BBC Active video footage. ActiveTeach allows you to play and customise lessons and import your own resources.

Grades in Get Ready

The grade descriptions in the 'Assess yourself' and 'ResultsPlus' features are designed to give students a general indication of the types of responses they need to produce in order to be likely to achieve particular grades when they start GCSE. The descriptions should always be considered in relation to the content outlined in the Edexcel specification.

Full colour lesson plans show exactly where resources from the student book and Active Teach could be used.

Practical suggestions and extra resources make the materials usable with all your students.

Advice in every lesson plan from NALDIC on how to help EAL students access the learning.

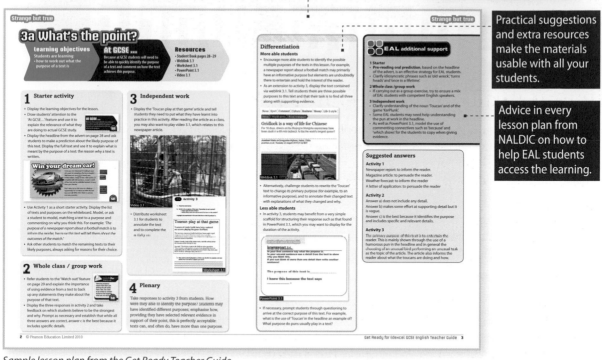

Sample lesson plan from the Get Ready Teacher Guide

A wealth of digital resources, including exclusive BBC Active footage.

Makes customisation easy by allowing you to play and re-order lessons and even incorporate your own tried-and-tested resources.

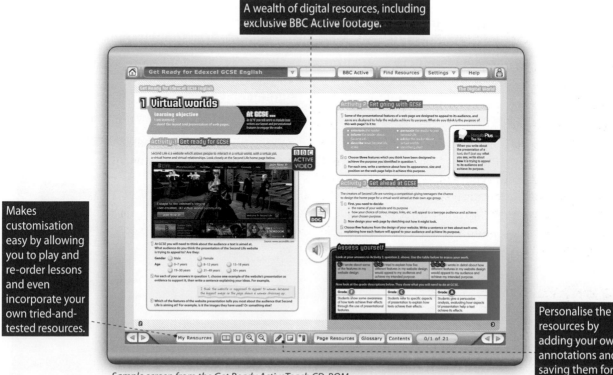

Sample screen from the Get Ready ActiveTeach CD-ROM

Personalise the resources by adding your own annotations and saving them for future use.

Unit 1
The Digital World

Recent years have seen a revolution in how we communicate with each other and access information.

▶ Before 2005, websites like YouTube did not even exist; by 2006 it was receiving 100 million hits a day; by 2010 this had risen to 2 billion hits a day!

▶ Social networking sites like MySpace have launched the careers of musicians such as the Arctic Monkeys and Lily Allen. They were even used by Barack Obama as part of his successful election campaign in the US.

▶ Similarly, Facebook launched in 2004 and is now the most popular social networking site with over 500 million users worldwide keeping in touch through status updates.

▶ More and more people are able to read books, magazines, newspapers and other texts online at the click of a button, using a variety of electronic and mobile devices.

▶ The digital revolution has created a whole new swathe of words and terms. Before 1998 people would have looked at you very oddly if you announced you were going to 'google' something. Likewise, words such as 'blog', 'wiki' and 'tweeting' are new terms that have come into use because of developments in digital communications.

In this unit you will encounter and read about the impact of the rapid growth of the digital world and consider some of the issues it has created. You will also get the chance to think about and develop your own ideas for digital texts.

LIFE   What Is Second Life?   World Map   Shopping   Buy Land   Community   Help   **Join Now »** It's fast, free and easy!

Escape to the Internet's largest user-created, 3D virtual world community.

Welcome To Second Life

Join Now »

What am I learning in this unit?

In this unit you will start to develop some of the following skills that you will need at GCSE.

Reading

I will learn how to:
- read and understand texts.
- comment on the structure and presentation of a text.
- work out what the purpose and audience of a text is.
- find and select bits of information from a text.
- use evidence from a text to support my points.
- comment on how a writer uses language for effect.
- compare two texts.

Writing

I will learn how to:
- gather ideas and how to plan a sequence for those ideas.
- vary my sentences so that my writing is more interesting for the reader.
- write in different forms.
- check my work and correct any mistakes.

Why do I need to know this?

All of the lessons in this unit focus on specific skills that you will eventually be assessed on during your GCSE English course. By practising and developing these skills now you can give yourself a head start so that when you do start GCSE you are prepared and ready to succeed!

1 Virtual worlds

Learning objective

I am learning:
- about the layout and presentation of web pages.

At GCSE ...

At GCSE you will need to explain how writers use layout and presentational features to engage the reader.

Activity 1 Get ready for GCSE

Second Life is a website which allows people to interact in a virtual world, with a virtual job, a virtual home and virtual relationships. Look closely at the Second Life home page below.

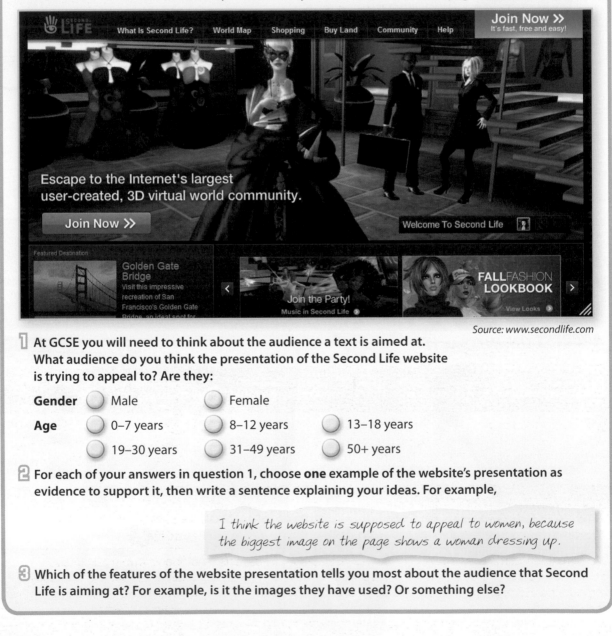

Source: www.secondlife.com

1   At GCSE you will need to think about the audience a text is aimed at. What audience do you think the presentation of the Second Life website is trying to appeal to? Are they:

Gender   ◯ Male   ◯ Female

Age   ◯ 0–7 years   ◯ 8–12 years   ◯ 13–18 years
         ◯ 19–30 years   ◯ 31–49 years   ◯ 50+ years

2   For each of your answers in question 1, choose **one** example of the website's presentation as evidence to support it, then write a sentence explaining your ideas. For example,

I think the website is supposed to appeal to women, because the biggest image on the page shows a woman dressing up.

3   Which of the features of the website presentation tells you most about the audience that Second Life is aiming at? For example, is it the images they have used? Or something else?

Activity 2 Get going with GCSE

1 Some of the presentational features of a web page are designed to appeal to its audience, and some are designed to help the website achieve its purpose. What do you think is the purpose of this web page? Is it to:

- **entertain** the reader
- **inform** the reader about Second Life
- **describe** what Second Life is like

- **persuade** the reader to join Second Life
- **advise** the reader about virtual worlds
- **something else?**

2 a Choose **three** features which you think have been designed to achieve the purpose you identified in question 1.

b For each one, write a sentence about how its appearance, size and position on the web page helps it achieve this purpose.

ResultsPlus
Top tip

When you write about the presentation of a text, don't just say **what** you see, write about **how** it is trying to appeal to its audience and achieve its purpose.

Activity 3 Get ahead at GCSE

The creators of Second Life are running a competition giving teenagers the chance to design the home page for a virtual world aimed at their own age group.

1 a First, you need to decide:
- the name of your website and its purpose
- how your choice of colour, images, links, etc. will appeal to a teenage audience and achieve your chosen purpose.

b Now design your web page by sketching out how it might look.

2 Choose **five** features from the design of your website. Write a sentence or two about each one, explaining how each feature will appeal to your audience and achieve its purpose.

Assess yourself

Look at your answers to Activity 3, question 2, above. Use the table below to assess your work.

👍 I wrote about some of the features in my website design.	👍👍 I tried to explain how five different features in my website design would appeal to my audience and achieve my intended purpose.	👍👍👍 I wrote in detail about how different features in my website design would appeal to my audience and achieve my intended purpose.

Now look at the grade descriptions below. They show what you will need to do at GCSE.

Grade **F**	Grade **C**	Grade **A**
Students show some awareness of how texts achieve their effects through the use of presentational features.	Students refer to specific aspects of presentation to explain how texts achieve their effects.	Students give a persuasive analysis, evaluating how aspects of presentation help a text achieve its effects.

2 The appeal of YouTube

Learning objective

I am learning:
• to look more closely at the audience and purpose of a text.

At GCSE ...

At GCSE you will need to identify the audience and purpose of a text so you can comment on how this has influenced the writer's choices.

YouTube is a website where you can watch and upload all kinds of videos. It was only created in 2005 but quickly became hugely popular. In 2006 Google bought YouTube for just over £1 billion!

Activity 1 Get ready for GCSE

1 What kind of audience do you think YouTube appeals to?

2 If you were creating a magazine or poster advert for YouTube, how would you appeal to this audience? Think about the images and the kind of language you would use.

3 Now look at the poster opposite. It was created by an advertising agency to make the point that everything that we now think of as modern will seem old-fashioned in the future.

   a How have the writer and designer of this poster made it seem old-fashioned? Think about:
      • the image
      • the fonts
      • the colours
      • the choice of language.

   b Write a short review of this poster explaining whether you think it will appeal to YouTube's audience or not.

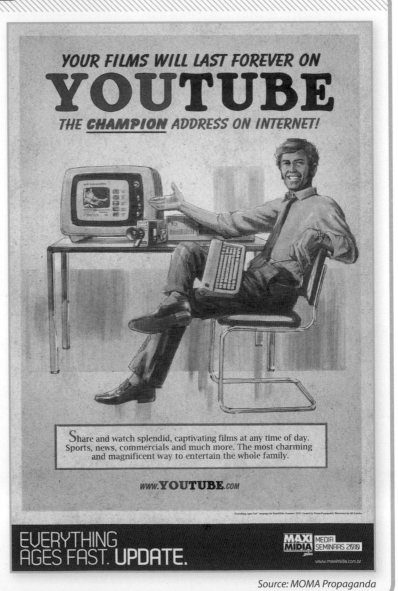

YOUR FILMS WILL LAST FOREVER ON
YOUTUBE
THE **CHAMPION** ADDRESS ON INTERNET!

Share and watch splendid, captivating films at any time of day. Sports, news, commercials and much more. The most charming and magnificent way to entertain the whole family.

www.**YOUTUBE**.com

EVERYTHING AGES FAST. **UPDATE.**

Source: MOMA Propaganda

Activity 2 Get going with GCSE

Look at how YouTube is described on its website.

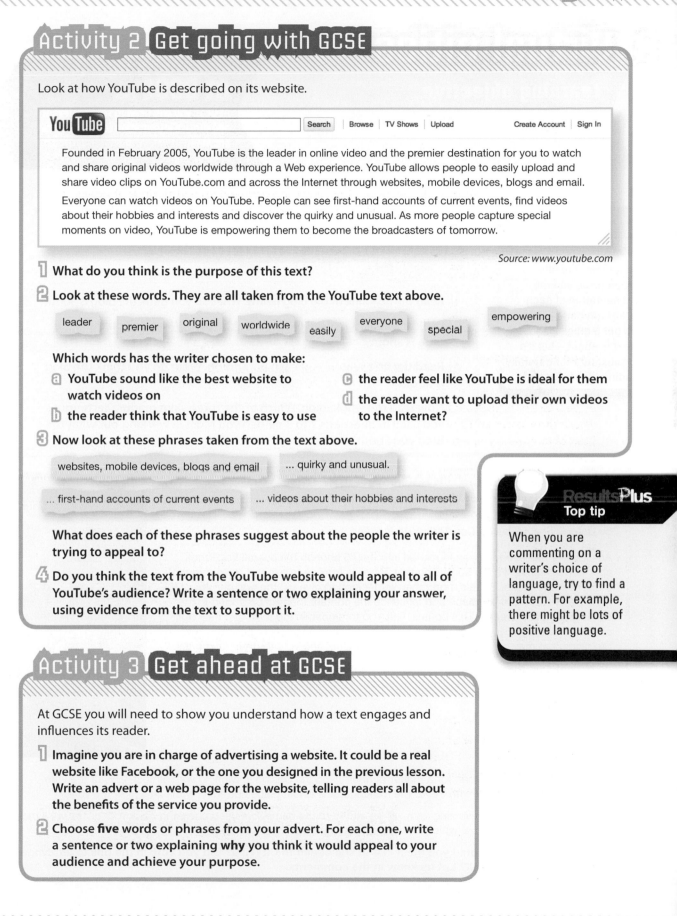

Founded in February 2005, YouTube is the leader in online video and the premier destination for you to watch and share original videos worldwide through a Web experience. YouTube allows people to easily upload and share video clips on YouTube.com and across the Internet through websites, mobile devices, blogs and email.

Everyone can watch videos on YouTube. People can see first-hand accounts of current events, find videos about their hobbies and interests and discover the quirky and unusual. As more people capture special moments on video, YouTube is empowering them to become the broadcasters of tomorrow.

Source: www.youtube.com

1 What do you think is the purpose of this text?

2 Look at these words. They are all taken from the YouTube text above.

leader   premier   original   worldwide   easily   everyone   special   empowering

Which words has the writer chosen to make:

a YouTube sound like the best website to watch videos on

b the reader think that YouTube is easy to use

c the reader feel like YouTube is ideal for them

d the reader want to upload their own videos to the Internet?

3 Now look at these phrases taken from the text above.

websites, mobile devices, blogs and email   ... quirky and unusual.

... first-hand accounts of current events   ... videos about their hobbies and interests

What does each of these phrases suggest about the people the writer is trying to appeal to?

4 Do you think the text from the YouTube website would appeal to all of YouTube's audience? Write a sentence or two explaining your answer, using evidence from the text to support it.

ResultsPlus
Top tip

When you are commenting on a writer's choice of language, try to find a pattern. For example, there might be lots of positive language.

Activity 3 Get ahead at GCSE

At GCSE you will need to show you understand how a text engages and influences its reader.

1 Imagine you are in charge of advertising a website. It could be a real website like Facebook, or the one you designed in the previous lesson. Write an advert or a web page for the website, telling readers all about the benefits of the service you provide.

2 Choose **five** words or phrases from your advert. For each one, write a sentence or two explaining **why** you think it would appeal to your audience and achieve your purpose.

3 Virtual cities

learning objective

I am learning:
• to use strategies to find key points and information from a text.

At GCSE ...

At GCSE you will need to select relevant and precise information to support your answers.

Skim reading is a way of picking out key bits of a text without reading every word of that text. It can help you read a text more quickly and understand what it is about.

ResultsPlus
Top tip

Remember: the title, any pictures and the first sentence of each paragraph can all help you get a quick idea what a text is about – but it's no substitute for carefully reading the whole text.

Activity 1 Get ready for GCSE

1. Read the headline of the blog below. What do you think the blog is about?

2. Look at the picture used to illustrate the blog. What do you think the blog is about?

3. Read the first sentence of each paragraph. What do you think the blog is about?

4. Now read the whole blog. Which of the three skim reading techniques you used in questions 1 to 3 helped you most in working out what the blog was about?

CityVille: Help choose which building(s) will be released next!

by Brandy Shaul, Posted Dec 14th 2010 8:10PM

1 As CityVille has already been launched into the #5 spot on the overall Facebook app leaderboards, it's not surprising that Zynga is looking to expand the amount of content in the game. What's more, they've decided to give us, the real players of the game, a chance to help shape and influence the content that will be added in the coming days and weeks. This comes, first and foremost, in the form of a new poll on the official CityVille forums, where users can look at a variety of possible new buildings that may or may not be added to the game, and vote for their favourites.

2 As of right now, there are just five buildings to choose from, and you'll need to log in to the forums in order to vote. The choices are:
Power Plant
Gas Station
Prison
Parking Lot
Casino

3 The post has only been open for a matter of hours, and the Casino is winning with almost 46% of the vote. Second is the gas station with 24%. The Parking Lot is in last place currently, with just 7% of the vote.

4 We don't know when the winning item will be added to the game, but keep checking back with us, as we'll make sure you're the first to know which item wins, and when we'll see it in the game.

5 Which of these items would you most like to see added to CityVille? Did you vote in the poll to let Zynga know your choice as well? Let us know in the comments.

Activity 2 | Get going with GCSE

When you are asked to answer questions about a text, you can scan the text for a key word from the question to help you find the information you need.

For example, to answer the question opposite you could run your eye over the text, looking for the key words 'app leaderboards'. You could also scan for numbers.

> According to the blog, what number is CityVille in the Facebook app leaderboards?

Results Plus
Watch out!

Be careful when you're scan reading: just because you've found the key word, it doesn't mean you've found the right answer. Check your answer actually answers the question!

1. Why do you think it is better to scan for the words 'app leaderboards' than, for example, the word 'number'?

2. Now scan the blog to find answers to the following questions. Write your answers out like the handwritten example:

   a. Who are the creators of CityVille, Zynga, giving a chance to influence the content that will be added to the game?

   b. Where do they have to go to vote in the poll?

   c. What are the choices in the vote?

   d. What is currently winning the vote and what is currently in last place?

According to the blog, CityVille is in the number five spot on the Facebook app leaderboards. (Key words: app leaderboards)

Activity 3 | Get ahead at GCSE

At GCSE you need to show you fully understand a text, so it is useful for you to be able to sum up the main points the writer is making.

1. For each of the five paragraphs in the blog, write **one** sentence of **up to 15 words** summing up what it is about.

2. Look carefully at your answer to question 1. Now write **one** sentence of **up to 15 words** summing up what the entire blog is about.

3. Compare your answers with a partner. Have you included all the most important information from the blog?

Assess yourself

Look at your answer to Activity 3, question 2. Use the table below to assess your work.

👍 I tried to sum up what the blog was about but I left out some important information.	👍👍 I summed up most of the important information in the blog.	👍👍👍 I clearly summed up the blog, including all key pieces of information.

Now look at the grade descriptions below. They show what you will need to do at GCSE.

Grade **F**	Grade **C**	Grade **A**
Students describe the main ideas from texts, using specific details from those texts.	Students understand the main ideas in a text, using specific details from those texts.	Students give persuasive interpretations of texts and choose apt quotations that support their points.

4 Social networking sites

learning objective

I am learning:
• to choose relevant evidence to support my points and comment on their effect.

At GCSE ...

At GCSE you must include examples from the text to support the points you make.

Social networking sites such as Facebook and MySpace are a relatively new form of digital text. They are a place where people can create profiles, join networks of friends and share information about themselves with others.

Activity 1 Get ready for GCSE

Read the newspaper article opposite. Then answer the questions below. You could use the skim reading techniques you practised in the previous lesson to help you.

Mail Online | Science & Tech

Home News Sport TV&Showbiz Femail Health **Science&Tech** Money Debate Coffee Break Property Motoring Travel

Science&Tech Home | Pictures | Gadgets Gifts and Toys Store | Login

Facebook users will be forced to change their names to escape cyber past, says Google boss

Comments (127) | Add to My Stories

Young people are exposing so much private information on social networking sites that they might have to change their identities in the future.

The chief executive of Google has warned users on sites such as Facebook may be
5 forced to change their names in order to escape their frivolous cyber past.

Eric Schmidt said the enormous quantity of detail left online by young users could come back to haunt them when they apply for jobs in future.

'I don't believe society understands what happens when everything is available, knowable and recorded by everyone all the time,' he told the *Wall Street Journal*.

10 Mr Schmidt's comments will fuel concerns about the amount of personal information made available online, most of which is virtually un-erasable.

An estimated 600 million people have personal online profiles, many of which are accessible to total strangers.

Prospective employers are able to access photographs, videos and blogs that users
15 may have long forgotten with a few simple clicks of a mouse.

Mr Schmidt's comments were welcomed by Internet experts.

Dylan Sharpe from the privacy website Big Brother Watch told the *Independent*, 'Right now there are millions of young kids and teenagers who, when they apply for jobs in ten years time, will find that there is so much embarrassing stuff about them
20 online that they cannot take down.'

'Undoubtedly we need to educate children, and many adults, for that matter, on the value of privacy.'

1 **Why does Eric Schmidt think that Facebook users may have to change their names in the future?**

2 **What do you think the writer means when she writes about the 'frivolous cyber past' of Facebook users (line 5)?**

3 **When and why does the article suggest this 'frivolous cyber past' will become a problem?**

Source: www.dailymail.co.uk

Activity 2 | Get going with GCSE

1 At GCSE you might be asked to pick out a number of key points about a text. What do you think are the **three** main points made in the newspaper article? Choose from the suggestions below – or use your own ideas.

- Young people are putting too much personal information on the Internet.
- People might have to change their names one day.
- Young people might regret what they have put on Facebook when they are looking for a job in the future.
- Prospective employers might be able to access your details.
- Lots of information people have put on the Internet cannot be deleted.

2 a Look at the quotations below taken from the newspaper article. Can you use either of them to support any of the three main points you selected in question 1?

> Prospective employers are able to access photographs, videos and blogs ...

> ... the enormous quantity of detail left online by young users could come back to haunt them.

b Now select quotations from the text to support the rest of the main points you chose in question 1.

Results Plus
Top tip

Always use a key word from the question in point-evidence-explanation paragraphs so you **know** you're answering the question.

Results Plus
Watch out!

At GCSE your points must be supported with evidence. If you can't find any evidence to support your point, it could be because it's wrong!

Activity 3 | Get ahead at GCSE

Look at this paragraph. It uses the point-evidence-explanation structure to answer the question:

> How has the writer of the article made this news story dramatic and disturbing?

The **evidence** to support the point

A key word from the question to make sure you are answering it

The article emphasises that what we do now on the Internet will be there for years in the future, maybe even forever. The writer says: 'the enormous quantity of detail left online by young users could come back to haunt them'. This suggests that young people might one day regret all the information they have put online. The word 'haunt' in particular makes it sound disturbing, as if it is a ghost that you cannot escape from.

The **point** you want to make

An **explanation** of the effect of this evidence on the reader

A comment on the writer's choice of language

1 Use the same paragraph structure to write your own answer to the question.

2 Annotate your paragraph with the same notes as the paragraph above. If you are missing any of these five key features of a successful point-evidence-explanation paragraph, try to add them in.

5 The power of the Internet

Learning objective

I am learning:
• how to make effective comments on the writer's choice of language.

At GCSE ...

At GCSE you will need to comment closely on how writers use language to get their ideas and perspectives across.

Activity 1 Get ready for GCSE

When Joe McElderry won *The X Factor* in 2009, everyone expected his first single to be the Christmas number one. Read the newspaper article below which explains what happened next.

| Home | News | Sport | **TV&Showbiz** | Femail | Health | Science&Tech | Money | Debate | Coffee Break | Property | Motoring | Travel |

TV&Showbiz Home | U.S. Showbiz | Headlines | A-Z Star Search | Pictures | Showbiz Boards | Blogs | Video | TV Listings   Login

Rage Against The Machine sells half a million copies to pip Joe McElderry (and Simon Cowell) to the Christmas No.1 spot

⊟ Comments (256) | ↧ Add to My Stories

The X Factor's stranglehold on the Christmas singles charts was dealt a devastating blow last night as Joe McElderry's bid for the No.1 spot was hijacked by a web campaign.

McElderry, this year's *X Factor* winner, was pipped to the post by American group Rage Against The Machine.

The group's **expletive-ridden** 1992 song 'Killing in the Name' sold more than half a million copies, beating the youngster's
5 cover of Miley Cyrus's 'The Climb' by 50,000 sales.

The news last night was described by industry experts as 'possibly the greatest chart upset ever' – but will delight record company Sony, who own the rights to both.

Geordie teen McElderry took the news graciously, writing on his Twitter page: 'Hey guys thank you to everybody that bought the single and supported me! Well done to RATM for an interesting chart battle.'

10 Essex couple Jon and Tracy Morter launched the 'Rage Against The Machine for Christmas No 1' Facebook site this month as a protest against *X Factor* chief Simon Cowell's dominance of the festive charts for the past four years.

It emerged last night that Cowell tracked down Mr Morter at the weekend and thanked him.

Mr Morter said yesterday: 'He was really nice and we had quite a discussion – he said he didn't mind what
15 we were doing – in fact he told me that he was grateful because it had made them all work that bit harder.'

Cowell, who was in the Caribbean last week, added last night: 'I am gutted for Joe because a No. 1 single meant a lot to him.'

McElderry said: 'This time last year I never thought for one minute that I'd win *The X Factor* never mind about having a debut single out, so I'm just delighted to be in the charts.'

Source: www.dailymail.co.uk

1 Look at some of the language the writer has used at the start of the article: stranglehold   devastating   hijacked

Why do you think the writer of this newspaper article used such dramatic language in the opening sentence?

2 Find another example of dramatic or **emotive** language used in the article. Explain the effect it has on the reader.

Glossary

expletive-ridden: full of bad language

Activity 2 Get going with GCSE

At GCSE you will need to look closely at the language writers use.

1. **Look at some of the language used to describe Joe McElderry in the article.**
   - We are told that he took the news of his defeat **graciously**
   - He is described as a **youngster**

   What impression do you think the writer is trying to give of McElderry?

2. **We are told that McElderry's song was** **pipped to the post** **by Rage Against The Machine's.** **What impression is the writer trying to give about Rage Against the Machine's victory?**

3. **Look at your answers in this activity so far. What does the writer's choice of language suggest about their attitude towards this chart battle? Use some of the quotations above to help explain your ideas.**

4. **Readers can look at articles like this on newspaper websites – and leave their own comments. Look at this example of a reader's online comment.**

Comments (256)

I feel sorry for Joe but not for Simon Cowell. He might run *The X Factor* but he doesn't rule the world. People can make up their own minds about the music they want to buy. Just because we've seen and heard him sing every week since September doesn't mean we're all going to rush out and buy the winner's song like a herd of sheep.

DM, Lincolnshire

What do you think? Write your own comment on the article, choosing your language carefully to get your points across.

Activity 3 Get ahead at GCSE

1. **You are going to write your own newspaper article about a Facebook campaign – real or imaginary.**

   a. **First, you need to plan your ideas by deciding:**
      - what the campaign was for (or against)
      - whether the campaign was successful or not
      - how the people involved felt about the campaign and the result.

   b. **Jot down some ideas about the kind of language you will use to describe:**
      - how the campaign worked
      - each of the people involved in the campaign.

   c. **Write your newspaper article.**

2. **Choose five different words from your article: ones which you used to create a particular effect. For each one, write a sentence explaining the effect you wanted that word to have on the reader.**

6 Comparing texts

Learning objective

I am learning:
• to compare two texts.

At GCSE ...

At GCSE you will be asked to compare the presentation, language choice and ideas in two different texts.

Activity 1 Get ready for GCSE

On pages 2–3 you explored the Second Life website. Like Second Life, Moshi Monsters is a virtual world. Members can adopt a monster and care for it by buying food, furniture, treats and toys, using virtual money earnt playing puzzle games.

Look at the home page of the Moshi Monsters website below.

Source: www.moshimonsters.com

1 a What audience do you think the presentation of the Moshi Monsters website is trying to appeal to? You could look at the list on page 2 to help you.

   b Choose **three** examples of the website's presentation as evidence, then write a sentence or two to explain why each example would appeal to this audience.

2 What do you think is the purpose of the Moshi Monsters home page? To persuade? To inform? To entertain? Or something else?

3 a How would you describe the language used on the Moshi Monsters home page?

   b Why do you think this kind of language will appeal to the website's target audience?

Activity 2 Get going with GCSE

In Activity 3 you are going to compare Second Life (page 2) and Moshi Monsters.

1. **The first things to do are to work out:**
   - Who is the **target audience** for each website – are they similar or different?
   - What is the **purpose** of each website – is it similar or different?

2. **Now you need to think about four key areas. For each of these four key areas, make notes about how the writers and designers have tried to achieve their intended purpose and appeal to their target audience. You could note your ideas in a table like the one below.**

	Use of colour	Choice of images	Choice of language	Layout
Second Life		Images of men and women suggest a website for adults.		
Moshi Monsters	Bright and colourful. suggests the site is aimed at children.			

3. **Now practise writing to compare the two texts using the choices below.**

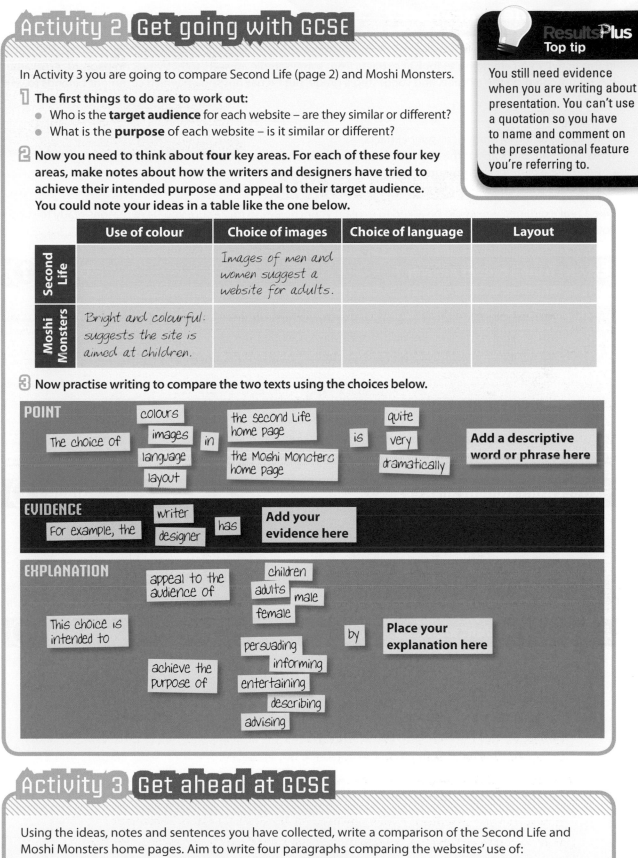

POINT

The choice of | colours / images / language / layout | in | the second Life home page / the Moshi Monsters home page | is | quite / very / dramatically | **Add a descriptive word or phrase here**

EVIDENCE

For example, the | writer / designer | has | **Add your evidence here**

EXPLANATION

This choice is intended to | appeal to the audience of | children / adults / male / female | by | **Place your explanation here**

achieve the purpose of | persuading / informing / entertaining / describing / advising

Activity 3 Get ahead at GCSE

Using the ideas, notes and sentences you have collected, write a comparison of the Second Life and Moshi Monsters home pages. Aim to write four paragraphs comparing the websites' use of:
- colour
- images
- language
- layout.

In this activity you are going to look at extracts from some sample answers to Activity 3 on page 13. An examiner has commented on the extracts and suggested a grade, but he has not shown which comment belongs to which extract.

Your task:
- Read the different student answer extracts.
- As you read, think about the strengths and weaknesses of the answers.
- Read the examiner's comments.
- Work out which comment belongs to which answer.

Like a real examiner, you could be asked to explain your choices so make sure you have reasons ready to support your answers.

Extract from student answer 1   Grade (?)

The language on the Moshi Monsters website is very clear and simple and tells the reader what to do. For example, it tells you to 'adopt a monster' or 'play games'. These are all things which would appeal to a younger audience and it uses strong persuasive language to get them to sign up for the website.

The language on the Second Life website is also clear. For example, it says 'Join now – it's fast, free and easy' but it also uses much more adult language than Moshi Monsters, for example, 'Escape to the Internet's largest user-created, 3D virtual world community'.

Extract from student answer 2   Grade (?)

The Second Life website is for adults and Moshi Monsters is for children. You can tell just by looking at them that one would make kids want to use it and kids wouldn't be interested in Second Life at all. There's nothing on it that would make them want to use it.

Extract from student answer 3   Grade (?)

Moshi Monsters is very colourful and has lots of cartoon characters. Second Life has pictures of adults and shows all the different things you can do on the website. For example you can change the way you look or go to a museum. I think this would appeal to adults because these are the kinds of things adults might want to do.

This extract from the student's answer is typical of E grade performance. The response shows understanding that the websites' audiences are different, but does not say anything about Second Life's target audience or support or develop the point with any evidence or explanation. If the student sustained this level throughout their response, it is likely that they would achieve a grade E.

This extract from the student's answer is typical of D grade performance. The response refers to a range of valid evidence but does not make a clear point or develop their analysis with comments on specific features of the texts. The comparison is limited, concentrating on the Second Life website, with little reference to the Moshi Monsters website. If the student sustained this level in the rest of their response, they would most likely achieve a grade D.

This extract from the student's answer is typical of C grade performance. The response uses a wide range of evidence and makes a clear comparison between the two websites. It looks closely at the ways in which the texts appeal to their audiences and how different features on each website might achieve this. This student is beginning to develop sound comments on the use of language. If the student sustained this type of writing throughout their response, they would probably achieve a grade C. A more fully developed comment on the use of language in the Second Life website would place this at the top of a grade C.

1 Now look at your own answer to this activity. Compare it to the three extracts from student answers on page 14.
   • Which one is your answer closest to?
   • Discuss or jot down what you might need to do to improve your answer if you were to do it again.

2 You have been asked to write an advice sheet for students who have never tackled this kind of question before and who are aiming for a grade C. Write your advice sheet, using some of the key words below.

layout   presentation

audience   purpose

image   colour   language

point   evidence   explanation   paragraphs

compare

7 For and against

Learning objective

I am learning:
• to take part in a group discussion.

At GCSE ...

At GCSE you will be assessed on how well you work in group discussions.

Social networking sites like Facebook have grown rapidly in size and have millions of users worldwide. However, not everyone thinks they are a good thing.

Activity 1 Get ready for GCSE

Read the newspaper article below.

Janet Street-Porter: Why I hate Facebook

1 Social networking site Facebook is five years old this week, but I won't be wasting time 'poking' cyber friends – that's contacting them to you and me – and celebrating online.

2 Nothing sums up the shallow world we live in more than a group of people chatting away to each other for hours each day via sites like Bebo, MySpace and Facebook.

3 Have these sad characters got nothing better to do? What is it about the real world that they find so unappealing?

4 Facebook has been a runaway success because it allows people to create their own profile and welcome new 'friends' with whom they can share their every waking thought.

5 Why do these people think we care about their lives? They spend hours boasting about what they've eaten, what they've watched on telly and who they fancy. Why do they shirk from real-life encounters?

6 What an irony that the site is called Facebook, because the one thing the site is not about is three-dimensional face-to-face confrontation. It's about whatever 'face' you decide to adopt online.

7 I worry that millions of people – and especially the young – may be losing the social skills they need to lead fulfilled lives, hold down a job and communicate effectively and honestly with their partners. In short, by logging on, they are tuning out of reality.

8 One of my pals recently told me he had joined a social networking site. I was **incredulous**. Secretly I thought: Is he so miserable with his real friends that he needs a load of nonjudgmental new ones? Has he no shame?

9 I don't need the **validation** of hundreds of cyber-friends on Facebook. And neither should anyone else.

Source: www.dailymail.co.uk

Glossary

incredulous: shocked, unable to believe it
validation: proof, confirmation or approval

1 a Make a list of all the arguments Janet Street-Porter makes against Facebook. For example,

• It's a waste of time.
• It's for people with nothing better to do.

b Can you think of any other reasons why people might think social networking sites like Facebook are a bad thing? Add them to your list.

2 Now make a list of all the reasons why people might think social networking websites are a good thing. For example, if you use Facebook, why do you like it? What benefits does it bring to your life?

Activity 2 Get going with GCSE

You are going to work in a group of four. Two members of your group will argue that Facebook is a good thing, and two will argue that it is not.

1. Working together, decide which two group members will argue that Facebook is a good thing and which two will argue that it is a bad thing.

2. Working with your partner, spend 2 or 3 minutes thinking about and noting down the points you want to make.

3. Copy the table below. As you carry out your discussion, each group member should complete a table like the one below, ticking off the skills each group member demonstrates during the discussion.

Group member	Made significant contributions ✓	Listened carefully ✓	Responded to others' ideas ✓

Results Plus
Watch out!

Listening is just as important as speaking. Concentrate on what the other people in your group are saying so you can respond to it.

Results Plus
Top tip

It's good to give your side of the argument – but even better if you can also say why your opponent's argument is wrong!

Activity 3 Get ahead at GCSE

1. Working as a group, give each member up to 1 minute to present their points to the rest of the group.

2. When everyone has had their chance to speak, you should discuss the issues and ideas that have been raised and try to come to a conclusion on which you can all agree. You may decide as a group that:
   - Facebook is a good thing
   - you hate Facebook
   - there are good and bad sides to Facebook.

   Write two or three sentences giving reasons to support your conclusion.

Assess yourself

Use the table below to assess how well you and the other members of your group did in this lesson.

👍 I listened sometimes and asked some questions.	👍👍 I listened carefully, responded to others and made contributions that helped the group come to a decision.	👍👍👍 I helped everyone think about each others' points and helped the group reach a final decision.

Now look at the grade descriptions below. They show what you will need to do at GCSE.

Grade F	Grade C	Grade A
Students listen with concentration and respond to others' ideas and opinions with relevant points.	Students listen carefully and make contributions that help develop their own and others' ideas.	Students take on different roles in discussions, always listening to others and making contributions that help move the discussion on.

8 Getting your ideas across

Learning objective

I am learning:
- to generate ideas and develop my planning skills.

At GCSE ...

For GCSE writing tasks you will need to plan and sequence your ideas to produce the best writing.

Thinking of ideas and planning how you are going to support and order those ideas is an essential skill at GCSE. Over the next few pages, you are going to plan, write and mark this GCSE-style writing task:

Write an article for a teenage magazine or a blog for a website aimed at teenagers with the title, 'Are social networking websites a waste of everybody's time?'

Activity 1 Get ready for GCSE

1. First of all you need to decide what you think. Do you agree or disagree: are social networking websites a waste of time? Write down four or five reasons why.

2. Now look at these two student plans for this task. Both students are arguing that social networking websites are **not** a waste of time:

Student A

- Facebook is really popular.
- It's fun.
- I use it all the time.
- There are some good games you can play.
- Even my mum uses it.

Student B

You can keep in touch with friends who live a long way away.

It helps people communicate with friends and family.

Social networking websites

You can make new friends.

You can get information about music you like.

People say it's addictive. It isn't – it's just good which is why people spend a long time on it.

Which plan do you think is better? Try to think of three or four reasons for your choice. It could be that:
- you prefer using bullet points or spider diagrams
- you think the ideas in one will make the article or blog more interesting than the other
- you think the points in one will answer the question better than the other
- something else.

3. Look at the reasons you wrote down in question 1 and make them into a plan. Can you think of any more points you could add?

Activity 2 Get going with GCSE

Once you have gathered all the points you want to make, you need evidence to support each one. You can use facts and statistics, something from your own experience or a quotation ... in fact anything which shows that your point is valid.

1 **Look at this point from Student B's plan on page 18.**

> You can keep in touch with friends who live a long way away.

Which of the following pieces of evidence do you think best supports this point?

a My friend emigrated to Australia and I've kept in touch with her on Facebook.

b More than 500 million people use Facebook so you can get in touch with almost anyone.

c My mum got in touch with her best friend from primary school on Facebook - she hadn't seen her for twenty-six years!

2 **Choose a piece of evidence to support each one of the points in your plan.**

ResultsPlus
Top tip

It's better to have too many ideas than too few. You can choose your best points and leave the weaker ones out.

Activity 3 Get ahead at GCSE

At GCSE, the best writing is often the result of good planning. Now you have chosen your points and found evidence to support each one, you need to put your points in the best order.

1 **Look at the sentence starters on the left that Student B included in his plan.**

Plan – sentence starters

a It helps people communicate with friends and family.

b You can keep in touch with friends who live a long way away.

c You can get information about music you like.

d You can make new friends.

e People say it's addictive. It isn't – it's just good which is why people spend a long time on it.

Connecting sentences

1 Not everyone thinks social networking websites are a good thing.

2 Another advantage of social networking is it gives you the chance to talk to people you would never meet in the real world.

3 However, Facebook doesn't just help you keep in touch with the people you see all the time.

4 Social networking isn't only about telling everyone what you had for dinner today.

a **What do you think would be the best order in which to put these five points?**

b **Now choose the best connecting sentence from the right to put in between each point.**

2 **Decide on the best order for the points in your own plan – and write connecting sentences to link them together.**

9 Adding variety

Learning objective

I am learning:
- to use different kinds of sentences to make my writing more interesting.

At GCSE ...

At GCSE your writing needs to show a variety of sentence structures.

Activity 1 Get ready for GCSE

Effective writing often uses different types of sentences. There are three basic types of sentence:

- simple sentences
- compound sentences
- complex sentences.

Simple sentences give the reader only one piece of information and contain only one verb. For example:

> verb
> I (love) the Internet.   I (chat) to my friends.   I (play) lots of games.

1. Think about the points and ideas you want to write in your magazine article or blog, 'Are social networking websites a waste of everybody's time?'

   a. Write **three** simple sentences which you could use.

   b. Check you have started each sentence with a capital letter and finished it with a full stop.

   c. Underline the verb in each sentence.

Activity 2 Get going with GCSE

You often find lots of simple sentences in writing for young children. To make your writing more mature and interesting, you should also use compound sentences.

Compound sentences are created by joining two simple sentences together, using a connective such as:  and but so

For example:

> verb   connective   verb
> I (chat) to my friends   (and)   I (play) lots of games.

1. a. Join these two simple sentences into one compound sentence using a connective.

   > I love the Internet.   My mum hates it.

   b. Look at these six simple sentences.

   | I want my own computer. | They are expensive. | I'm asking for a laptop for Christmas. |

   | I won't get one. | I'll have to save up. | It could take years. |

   Sort them into pairs and join them with a connective to make compound sentences.
   How many different compound sentences can you make?

Activity 2 continued...

2 You can also add information to simple sentences by creating complex sentences which are made up of two pieces of information called the **main clause** and the **subordinate clause**. They are joined together with a connective such as:

if   when   although   because   unless

For example:

| Teenagers love Facebook | because | you can keep in touch with your friends. |

This is the main clause. It makes sense by itself.   connective   This is the subordinate clause. It doesn't really make sense without the main clause.

Look at these six simple sentences.

I spend a lot of time on Facebook.   I do other things as well.

My parents worry.   I want to keep in touch with my friends.

I have lots of Facebook friends.   Adults don't understand.

Sort them into pairs and join them with a connective to make complex sentences. How many different complex sentences can you make?

ResultsPlus
Top tip

If you keep using the same connectives, it makes your writing sound really repetitive. When you've finished writing, check for words you've used twice – and change them.

Activity 3 Get ahead at GCSE

The paragraph below is written using only simple sentences. Re-write it so it includes some compound and complex sentences, and a variety of connectives.

Many people lose touch with their friends. Social networking sites can help with this. They allow people to communicate with each other anywhere in the world. For example, I did not see my best friend from primary school for three years. She moved to another school. I signed up for Facebook. I talk to her every day now. This is just one of the positive things about social networking sites. We may spend a long time on them. It is not necessarily wasted time.

Assess yourself

Look at the paragraph you wrote for Activity 3. Use the table below to assess your work.

| 👍 I used simple sentences and some compound sentences. | 👍👍 I used a range of all three sentence types. | 👍👍👍 I used a range of sentence types and connectives. |

Now look at the grade descriptions below. They show what you will need to at GCSE.

Grade F	Grade C	Grade A
Students use mainly simple and compound sentences, but do include some complex sentences.	Students use a range of sentence structures in their writing, formed accurately.	Students use a range of sentence structures accurately and for deliberate effect.

10 Language and audience

Learning objective

I am learning:
• to match my choice of language to the audience.

At GCSE ...

At GCSE you will be assessed on how well the language in your writing shows awareness of the audience you are writing for.

Activity 1 Get ready for GCSE

Look at the sentence below. It's taken from a website advising children aged 5–7 how to use the Internet safely.

> We've made this website to help you go on the Internet in a safe way and know who to talk to if you are worried.

Source: www.thinkuknow.co.uk

1 How is the language in this sentence appropriate for its audience?

2 Look at these three extracts from a thesaurus. Using these extracts, re-write the sentence above so that its language is more appropriate for:
- a website for adults using the Internet for the first time
- a website for teenagers.

Made	Talk to	Worried
created	approach	anxious
constructed	contact	concerned
established	converse with	perturbed
produced	consult	troubled

Results Plus
Top tip

You know thousands of words – and your first choice may not be your best choice. When you're checking your work, look out for vocabulary you can improve to make your meaning clearer, and your writing more appropriate to your audience.

Activity 2 Get going with GCSE

At GCSE you will also need to make sure your language is appropriate to the situation you are in and the relationship you want to create with your reader.

1 Imagine you meet someone you know in the street.

a How would you greet them if it was:
- a friend
- your head teacher
- your mum
- your friend's mum?

b Write a sentence explaining why you would greet these people in different ways – and what would happen if, for example, you spoke to your head teacher in the same way as your friend.

Activity 2 continued...

2 People wear different clothes for different occasions. For example, for a job interview you would wear **formal** clothes but at the weekend you would wear **informal** clothes.

You have been invited to:

a an awards ceremony at your community centre celebrating local heroes

b a wedding

c your friend's house

d dinner at your neighbour's house.

Put these events in order, according to how formal your outfit would be: from the most formal to the most informal.

3 Now think about the kind of language you would expect from these different texts:

a The head of Year 9 talking in assembly about the use of social networking websites.

b A magazine article for teenagers about the use of social networking websites.

c A student texting another student about the use of social networking websites.

d A letter from a head teacher to parents about students' use of social networking websites.

Which do you think would be the most formal? Put them in order, from the most formal to the most informal.

4 Look at the sentences on the right. They are taken from the texts you thought about in question 3.

a Match each sentence to the correct text.

b How did you work it out? Write down one or two words from each text which helped you identify it.

1 iv put fotos from party on fb haha! spk l8r x

2 One or two of you may not use Facebook and the like. But I know most of you spend half your time on them.

3 It has come to my attention that a significant minority of students have become involved in a campaign organised via a social networking website.

4 For the average teenager, Facebook is like food – you're not quite sure how you'd survive without it.

Activity 3 Get ahead at GCSE

At GCSE your choice of language will need to show you are aware of the right level of formality for the text you are writing and the audience you are writing for.

1 Look again at the sentences you wrote for Activity 3, question 2, page 17.

a Re-write them, making your language choice as **formal** as possible.

b Re-write them, making your language choice as **informal** as possible.

c Re-write them, making your language choice **appropriate** for a magazine article or blog aimed at teenagers.

11 On form

learning objective

I am learning:
• to explore the structure of different forms of writing.

At GCSE ...

At GCSE you might be asked to write in different forms, so you need to have knowledge of the structure of these forms.

Activity 1 Get ready for GCSE

1. Who is your favourite band or singer? Imagine you have just heard their latest song. You are going to tell people what you think about it.

   a. Text a friend. Remember, you can't use more than 140 characters.

   b. Write a comment to go on a friend's Facebook wall.

   c. Write a short review of around 100 words to post on a music review website.

   d. Write a script for a music review TV programme.

2. What differences can you see in these four pieces of writing? Think about:
   - the kind of words you have used
   - the amount you have written
   - how you have organised your ideas

3. At GCSE, you may be asked to write in forms such as a letter, a podcast, a blog, a newspaper or magazine article, or a leaflet.

   a. Choose **three** of these forms.

   b. What differences are there between the way they are set out and structured? Make a list of as many differences as you can think of. You could write your answers in a table like the one below.

Letter	Newspaper article	Blog
• No pictures • Your address and the address you're writing to	• A picture or two	• Contain links to related blogs • Contributions grouped by date/topic

Activity 2 Get going with GCSE

Although there are some differences in form, most extended non-fiction texts (things like magazine articles and letters) are organised in the same way:

Introduction: this explains to the reader why you are writing and what you are writing about.

Main body: this explores your ideas and opinions in detail.

Conclusion: this sums up your ideas and opinions.

1. **Look back at the short review you wrote in Activity 1c. If you included an introduction, write a sentence or two explaining its purpose: how did it help the reader? If you didn't include an introduction, add one now.**

2. **Look again at the task you have been preparing for.**

   Write an article for a teenage magazine or a blog for a website aimed at teenagers with the title, 'Are social networking websites a waste of everybody's time?'

   a Which of these ideas do you think would make a good introduction to your article?

   Some facts about social networking websites: how many people use them?

   Parents often think social networking websites are a waste of time.

   Some facts about how long people spend on social networking websites.

   A short history of all the main social networking websites.

   An explanation of what a social networking website is.

   b Choose two or three ideas to include in your introduction. You could use some of the ideas above, or some of your own, or both.

3. **Your conclusion is the last thing your reader will read. So it's the last chance you have to make an impression on them, and to influence their thoughts and ideas.**

   a What do you want your reader to be thinking as soon as they have finished reading your article?

   b Write the conclusion to your article: two or three sentences that will make the reader think what you want them to think.

ResultsPlus
Top tip

Always plan your conclusion **before** you start writing. You need to know where you're going if you want an easy, comfortable journey.

ResultsPlus
Watch out!

Your conclusion should sum up your ideas and leave the reader thinking. It should **not** be just a summary, repeating everything you have already written!

Activity 3 Get ahead at GCSE

Now you have planned the ideas for the main body of your article, your introduction and your conclusion, you are ready to start writing. Remember:

- You have spent a long time planning your article – so keep referring to your plan as you write.
- You are writing for a teenage magazine – so choose your language to suit your audience.
- Every point you make in the main body of your article should be supported with evidence and explanation.
- Really good writing uses a variety of sentence types and connectives.

12 An eye for detail

Learning objective

I am learning:
• to proofread and improve my work.

At GCSE ...

At GCSE you will need to spend time checking and improving your work so that it is the best it can be.

Checking your work is a vital part of writing at GCSE, but it is one of the things that students often forget to do. If you get into the routine now of leaving some time to check your work, then this will help you when you start GCSE.

Activity 1 Get ready for GCSE

Look at this paragraph from one student's magazine article.

> Some people say Facebook is addictive. They say that once you go on Facebook you can spend hours on it. You read what people have written on your wall and you write on someone else's wall and then you maybe play a game and then you have a look at your friends' photos and add some more of your own photos and then it's time to check your wall again and maybe write on someone else's wall. I sometimes spend two or three hours a night on it. At the weekends I can spend a whole afternoon on it. And sometimes the evening as well. It's not that it's addictive. It's just that there's lots you can do and all of it's interesting and fun and sociable and fun.

1. **What do you think this student has done well? And what could they improve? First, think about these two key areas of proofreading:**
   • **Organisation:** has the writer used point-evidence-explanation to structure the paragraph?
   • **Written expression:** is the writing clear and interesting? Or does it repeat itself and make the same point over and over again?

   Write a sentence or two explaining what you think the writer has done well and what could be improved in these two key areas.

2. **Re-write the paragraph above, making the improvements you noted in question 1.**

Activity 2 Get going with GCSE

Now look at this paragraph from another student's blog.

> The world can be a dangrous place for young people. Parents worry if there children our not home before dark. Yet in winter in the UK this is at 4 o'clock in the afternoon how can young people improve their social skills if they cannot see their friends after school? With the inventon of social networking on the Internet this is not a problem anymore now young people can keep in touch with their friends and their parents dont get a huge phone bill at the end of it. The only qestion is, why are parents complaining.

Activity 2 continued...

1 **What do you think this student has done well? And what could they improve? Think about these two key areas of proofreading:**
   - **Spelling:** has the writer spelt most words correctly, getting only the more difficult ones wrong? Or are there careless mistakes, for example the same word spelt in two different ways?
   - **Punctuation:** has the writer used full stops and question marks correctly?

   Write a sentence or two explaining what you think the writer has done well and what could be improved in these two key areas.

2 **Re-write the paragraph, making the improvements you noted in question 1.**

Activity 3 | Get ahead at GCSE

1 **Look at the magazine article or blog you have written. Working on your own or with a partner, use the table below to note down the areas you could improve with careful proofreading.**

		✓ or X		✓ or X
Organisation	My article/blog has an introduction at the beginning and a conclusion at the end.		All the paragraphs in the main body are structured using point-evidence-explanation.	
Written expression	All my writing makes clear sense to the reader.		I haven't repeated myself or made the same point over and over again.	
Sentence variety	I have used a range of different sentence types: simple, compound and complex.		I have used a range of sentence lengths: some short and some longer.	
Spelling	I have checked all the spellings I'm not sure about.		I've checked the spellings that are easy to get wrong, e.g. there, their and they're; to, too and two.	
Punctuation	I've used capital letters at the start of all my sentences and full stops at the end.		I haven't used commas where I should have used full stops.	

2 **Concentrating on each of the five key areas above, one at a time, make your magazine article as well and accurately written as you possibly can.**

ResultsPlus
Top tip

Check your work for one thing at a time: organisation, written expression, then check the sentence variety and so on. If you try and do it all at once, you'll miss lots of errors.

In this activity you are going to look at extracts from some sample answers to Activity 3 on page 25. An examiner has commented on the extracts and suggested a grade, but he has not shown which comment belongs to which answer.

Your task:
- To read the different student answer extracts.
- As you read, think about the strengths and weaknesses of the answers.
- Read the examiner's comments.
- Work out which comment belongs to which extract.

Like a real examiner, you could be asked to explain your choices so make sure you have reasons ready to support your answers.

Extract from student answer 1   Grade (?)

When your a teenager your friends are some of the most important people in your life. Communicating with them helps you develop the social skills you will use as an adult – in your family relationships, your work relationships and your social life. Employers often say that communication skills are the most important thing in lots of jobs. So as well as being fun and a really good way to comunicate with your friends, Facebook is helping us teenagers get ready for the big wide world.

Extract from student answer 2   Grade (?)

There are one hundred and sixty eight hours in a week and you can't spend all of them working and learning and doing something useful, I spend a lot of time playing football, talking to my friends, going out, and going on Facebook. I'm not learning anything or earning any money but who would call enjoying yourself a waist of time?

Extract from student answer 3   Grade (?)

Facebook is not a wast of time becuase there are lots of things you can do on it you can write messages and look at fotos and see what all your friends have written. Its better for teens to be on facebook than out doing vandelism or something because at least it doesnt do eny harm unless someone rites something bad on your wall that can upset you. Sometimes people get in truble for doing that.

This extract from the student's answer is typical of E grade performance. The response shows understanding of the purpose of the article, but loses focus on the main issue of whether social networking sites are a waste of time. There are a number of significant spelling and punctuation errors, in particular the use of very long sentences held together with a large number of connectives. Two or three shorter sentences would be more effective. If the rest of the answer had been of the same standard, it is likely that it would have achieved a grade E.

This extract from the student's answer is typical of D grade performance. The student expresses their argument powerfully, using evidence from their own experience. It is written with awareness of audience and purpose. Spelling of a limited vocabulary is generally sound but punctuation needs some attention, particularly the use of a comma to join two sentences where a full stop is needed. If the student sustained this type of writing throughout their response, they would probably achieve a grade D.

This extract from the student's answer is typical of C grade performance. The student is clearly aware of the purpose of the task and shows some awareness of the intended audience. The writer uses a well structured paragraph, with some convincing evidence used to support the point being made. Written expression is generally sound with few errors in spelling and punctuation. If the student sustained this level in the rest of their response, they would most likely achieve a grade C. A broader choice of vocabulary would help push this answer further into the grade C boundaries.

Choose one of the three answer extracts on page 28. Using the examiner's comments, try to improve the answer.

1 Now look at your own answer to this activity. Compare it to the three extracts from student answers on page 28.
   • Which one is your answer closest to?
   • Discuss or jot down what you might need to do to improve your answer if you were to do it again.

2 You have been asked to write an advice sheet for students who have never tackled this kind of question before and who are aiming for a grade C. Write your advice sheet, using some of the key terms below.

purpose   audience   structure   paragraphs

vocabulary   spelling   punctuation   evidence

sentence structure

Unit 2
Strange But True

The world of news and media can sometimes be a very strange and peculiar place, throwing up absurd and interesting stories, events and ideas. Just look at some of the headlines of texts you are going to encounter in this unit:

Pigeon post beats broadband

The real RAM raider

Inventor uses suction to crawl up a wall, Spider-Man-style

Mystery of man wearing horse's head

In this unit you will read about some of the strange but true stories that appear in the news and media, looking at how writers create these texts for maximum effect. You will also get the chance to write your own 'strange but true' text about something surprising or amazing that might have happened in your local area.

What am I learning in this unit?

In this unit you will start to develop some of the following skills that you will need at GCSE.

Reading

I will learn how to:
- read and understand texts.
- comment on the structure and presentation of a text.
- work out what the writer's point of view is.
- analyse how the writer uses language to get their point of view across.
- understand how a writer chooses language to change the way readers react to texts.
- understand how images, including moving images, contribute to the overall effect of a text.
- develop my comments on a text in more detail in order to improve my responses.
- compare two texts.

Writing

I will learn how to:
- write for different purposes – for example to inform, to describe or to persuade.
- structure my writing in different ways so it has the most impact.
- vary the length of my sentences for effect.
- write an extended article.
- check my work and correct any mistakes.

Speaking and listening

I will learn how to:
- prepare and present a talk on a given subject.

Why do I need to know this?

All of the lessons in this unit focus on specific skills that you will eventually be assessed on when you start GCSE English. By practising and developing these skills now you can give yourself a head start so that when you do start GCSE you are prepared and ready to succeed!

1 Get the picture

Learning objective
I am learning:
• to explore the impact and effect of images in texts.

At GCSE …
At GCSE you will need to comment on the choice of images in non-fiction and media texts.

Newspaper and magazine articles often include images. Not only do they give the reader more information, they affect the readers response to the text.

Activity 1 Get ready for GCSE

Look at the image below. It was used to illustrate one of the newspaper articles opposite.

Study the image, read the newspaper articles and then answer the questions below.

Article A

The real-life Sleeping Beauty

She is known to her family and friends as 'Sleeping Beauty' – but her life is no fairytale. Louisa Ball, 15, sleeps for two weeks at a time because she suffers from an incredibly rare disorder.

Article B

My kids are lazy little slobs – why DO I let them get away with it?

My eldest will Hoover if I nag him. My youngest son will wash up but, at five, he's not very good at it and I have to do it again. My middle son … will … cook … just because he likes it … Most of the time, they sit on their lazy bottoms doing nothing.

Article C

Giving teenage pupils a lie-in can boost their exam results

Giving pupils an hour's lie-in each morning boosts brainpower and cuts absenteeism, a pioneering scheme has found. The traditional 9am starts at Monkseaton High School were pushed back to 10am six months ago, in the wake of research showing teenagers' body clocks are slower than those of adults.

1 a Which article do you think the image was used to illustrate? Write a sentence or two explaining your answer.

b What do you think was the purpose of the image?

2 Look at the image again. As a reader, how would you respond to the image if it were used to illustrate:

a Article A?

b Article B?

c Article C?

Activity 2 | Get going with GCSE

The reader's response to Article A, the story of the real-life Sleeping Beauty, might be different if one of the images below had been chosen to illustrate it.

Image A

Image B

1 Look at these comments made by GCSE students.

  a Which comments were made about which images, do you think?

  b Which comments do you agree with? Write a sentence or two explaining your answer.

2 Look again at Image A above. How does the caption opposite change your reaction to the image?

Student A

The picture makes you feel more sorry for the girl because she looks so normal with her family

Student B

The picture gives it a light-hearted tone, as though they are making a joke.

Student C

She looks fine which makes her condition seem less serious.

Student D

It makes you think the story might not be real.

Scared: *Louisa with father Richard and mother Lottie, who said her condition turned her into a different person*

Activity 3 | Get ahead at GCSE

1 Look again at Article B in Activity 1.

  a Describe the photo you would choose to illustrate this article.

  b What effect will your chosen image have on the reader? Write a sentence or two explaining your answer.

2 Look again at Article C in Activity 1.

  a Describe the photo you would choose to illustrate this article.

  b What effect will your chosen image have on the reader? Write a sentence or two explaining your answer.

ResultsPlus
Top tip

When commenting on an image don't just say that it 'illustrates' the text. Think about how the image **reinforces** the writer's point of view as well as the effect it might have on the reader.

2 Moving images

Learning objective

I am learning:
- to explore the impact and effect of moving images.

At GCSE ...

At GCSE you will need to comment on the selection and presentation of images in a media text in your controlled assessment.

Activity 1 Get ready for GCSE

The images below are taken from a television trailer for the BBC series, *Being Human*. Look at the images and read the captions.

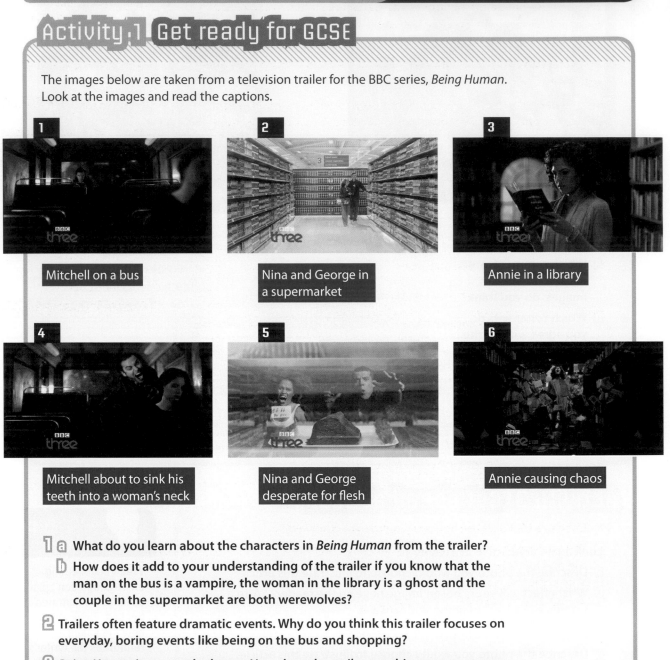

1 Mitchell on a bus

2 Nina and George in a supermarket

3 Annie in a library

4 Mitchell about to sink his teeth into a woman's neck

5 Nina and George desperate for flesh

6 Annie causing chaos

1 a What do you learn about the characters in *Being Human* from the trailer?

   b How does it add to your understanding of the trailer if you know that the man on the bus is a vampire, the woman in the library is a ghost and the couple in the supermarket are both werewolves?

2 Trailers often feature dramatic events. Why do you think this trailer focuses on everyday, boring events like being on the bus and shopping?

3 *Being Human* is a comedy drama. How does the trailer get this message across to the audience?

Activity 2 Get going with GCSE

1. At first the characters seem to be ordinary people – then suddenly they start to behave strangely.

   a. What is your first impression of these characters?

   b. How does this change by the end of the trailer?

2. Some of the characters' actions in the trailer are shown in slow motion – and some at normal speed. What effect do you think the makers of the trailer wanted to achieve?

3. The song *Can't Keep It In* is played during the trailer. Why do you think the trailer makers chose this song?

4. At the end of the trailer, the characters stop behaving strangely and start behaving like ordinary people again. What is the effect of this sudden change?

5. Think about the different elements of this trailer and the effect they have. Match the elements to their effects. Note that some elements have more than one effect and that some effects may be created by more that one element.

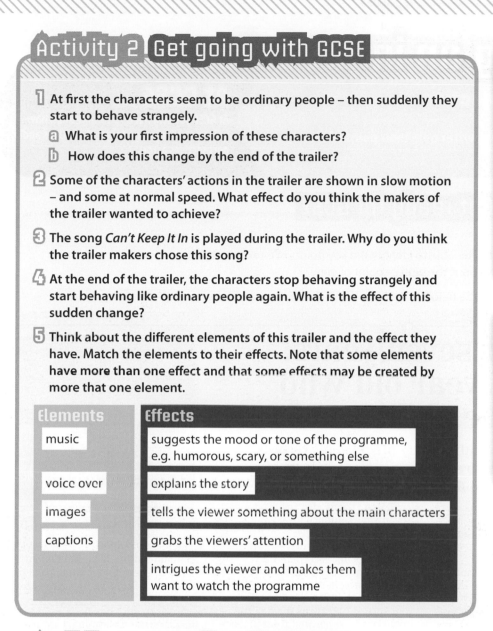

Elements	Effects
music	suggests the mood or tone of the programme, e.g. humorous, scary, or something else
voice over	explains the story
images	tells the viewer something about the main characters
captions	grabs the viewers' attention
	intrigues the viewer and makes them want to watch the programme

Results Plus
Watch out!

Everything in a media text has been chosen for its effect. Don't just write what it's about or what the characters say. Think about the music, the position and angle of the camera, the on-screen captions, and anything else you can see or hear.

Results Plus
Top tip

The more you watch a moving image text, the more you will notice. Watch a text you are trying to analyse three or four times before you try writing about it.

Activity 3 Get ahead at GCSE

1. a. Choose a film or television programme you know well.

   b. You have been asked to make a trailer to advertise it. Create a storyboard, like the one for *Being Human* in Activity 1, showing the key images, dialogue, setting and music that you will use in your trailer.

   As you plan your trailer, remember all the different things that you are trying to get across to your audience:

   - what the programme or film is about
   - what the characters are like
   - the mood of the film or television programme

   Above all, you need to intrigue the viewer and grab their attention so that they will definitely want to watch the film or programme you are advertising.

3 Making an impression

learning objective

I am learning:
• to work out how a writer gets their point of view across.

At GCSE ...

At GCSE you will need to comment on how writers use language to get their ideas and perspectives across.

Activity 1 Get ready for GCSE

At GCSE you will need to be able to identify the key points in a text and think about what they show about the writer's point of view.

Read the newspaper article below, then answer the questions that follow it.

Jailed for seven years: the eight year old who stole three shillings

The release of nineteenth century prison ships records reveal how young children were imprisoned alongside murderers, thieves and **bigamists**.

1 Ships used as floating prisons were intended to help overcrowding in traditional jails, according to the Prison Hulk Registers and Letter Books, 1802–1849.

2 The inmates of these prison hulks, as they were known, were aged from eight to 84 years old according to records held by the National Archives in Kew and now available online.

3 The records show that young children were kept locked up with murderers, thieves and bigamists. Francis Creed, for example, was jailed for seven years for stealing three shilling's worth of copper.

4 Samuel Philips was jailed for life at the age of 16 having been convicted of burglary.

5 William Davies also received a seven year sentence for stealing sheep at the age of 84.

6 Whether William survived his sentence is not recorded. Each prison ship could house between 200 and 300 prisoners in such cramped conditions that disease was **rife** and spread quickly as the healthy could not be separated from the sick. Approximately one in every three prisoners died before the end of their sentence aboard the disease-ridden ships.

7 Earlier this year, David Cameron suggested prison ships could once again be a simple, 'cost effective' way of adding to the capacity of Britain's crowded jails.

8 Politicians and campaigners widely condemned the idea, the Labour party arguing that it would cost far more than building new prisons on land.

9 A prison ship has been used to house Britain's criminals as recently as 2005, when HMP *The Weare* was sold after eight years' use as a floating jail off the coast of Dorset.

10 It was taken out of use shortly after the Chief Inspector of Prisons reported it to be unfit for purpose due to prisoners' restricted access to fresh air and exercise.

Glossary

bigamist: someone who marries again while still married to someone else
rife: widespread

1 a Why were prison ships introduced in the nineteenth century and why did David Cameron suggest re-introducing them in 2010?

   b What kinds of crimes were people imprisoned for in the nineteenth century?

2 What impression does the article give you of prison ships? Write two or three sentences explaining your ideas.

Activity 2 Get going with GCSE

At GCSE you will need to do more than just say what the writer's perspective is; you will need to back up what you say with evidence from the text.

Look closely at the first sentence of the newspaper article:

Look at how the writer has made their opinion clear from the very beginning of the article:

> The release of nineteenth century prison ships records reveal how young children were imprisoned alongside murderers, thieves and bigamists.

- We're told that young children were imprisoned on prison ships.
- We're told that they were kept with older and more dangerous criminals.

1 **Identify three other details which the writer has chosen to include in the article to emphasise their point of view. Think about:**
   - the kind of people who were imprisoned on these ships, their ages, and their crimes
   - the conditions on board these ships
   - the reasons we no longer have prison ships.

ResultsPlus
Top tip

When you have found three or four pieces of evidence which tell you about the writer's ideas, don't just think about them one by one. Consider the overall effect of all of them.

Activity 3 Get ahead at GCSE

1 **Imagine it is the twenty-third century. You have to write a description of UK schools in the twenty-first century for a newspaper article. Look at the advice opposite and then write your article.**

Remember to:
- decide on your point of view before you start writing: will your description be positive, negative or somewhere in between?
- choose descriptive language which supports your point of view
- choose details which support your point of view.

2 **Look carefully at your own or a partner's description. Write a paragraph or two about how your partner's choice of language and detail reflects his or her point of view.**

Assess yourself

Look at your answers to Activity 2. Use the table below to assess your work.

👍 I wrote clearly about some of the writer's ideas.	👍👍 I wrote clearly about the writer's ideas, using evidence from the text.	👍👍👍 I wrote in detail about the writer's ideas, using evidence from the text.

Now look at the grade descriptions below. They show you what you will need to do at GCSE.

Grade **F**	Grade **C**	Grade **A**
Students show some awareness of how writers achieve their effects through their use of language.	Students refer to specific aspects of language to explain how writers achieve their effects.	Students give a persuasive analysis, evaluating how aspects of language help writers achieve their effects.

4 Supporting a point of view

Learning objective

I am learning:
• to analyse how the choice of language and evidence help the writer to express their point of view.

At GCSE...

At GCSE you will need to comment on the techniques writrs use to support their point of view.

Activity 1 Get ready for GCSE

Read the newspaper article below, then answer the questions which follow it.

HOME	NEWS	SPORT	FINANCE	LIFESTYLE	COMMENT	TRAVEL	CULTURE	TECHNOLOGY	FASHION	Jobs	Dating	Offers

Technology News | Technology Companies | Technology Reviews | Video Games | Start-Up 100 | Technology Blogs | Technology Video

Pigeon post beats broadband

1 Ten pigeons carrying USB keys flew 120 miles from a farm in Yorkshire to Skegness in an hour and a quarter on Thursday.

2 At the moment the birds were released, a five-minute video upload to YouTube was started. By the time the pigeons reached their destination, only 24 per cent of a 300**MB** file had uploaded.

3 The stunt was part of a campaign to show how slow Internet connections can be in some parts of the UK.

4 A similar experiment was carried out in Durban, South Africa, last year. A pigeon named Winston completed a 96km flight in just two hours. Meanwhile, only 4 per cent of a 4**GB** file had uploaded.

5 Tref Davies of internet service provider Timico, who organised the stunt said, 'The farm we are using has a connection of around 100 to 200 **Kbps** (kilobits per second). This is the UK. It should be well-connected but around a third of homes still can't get broadband.'

6 British Telecom disputes this figure. A spokesperson said that 99 per cent of homes in the UK could now get broadband and only an estimated 160,000 households were unable to access the service due to 'excessive line length' meaning that 'broadband won't work.'

7 The BBC commissioned research last year which suggested that approximately three million homes in the UK had Internet connections operating at less than 2**Mbps** (megabits per second).

8 The government has undertaken to deliver a minimum of 2Mbps to every home by 2015.

Glossary

MB, GB: megabyte, gigabyte – unit used to show the size of an electronic file
Kbps, Mbps: kilobits, megabits per second – a measurement of the speed of an Internet connection

1 Why did the campaigners release the pigeons and what point did they want to make?

2 Look at paragraph 5. What is Tref Davies's point of view?

3 Look at paragraph 6. What is British Telecom's point of view?

4 Read the article again. Are there any clues which tell you about the writer's point of view? Do you think he is happy with the speed of Internet connections in Britain?

Activity 2 | Get going with GCSE

At GCSE you need to comment on how words and phrases reveal the writer's point of view.

1 **Look at the language which the writer uses to describe this event:** experiment   stunt

Now look at these dictionary definitions:

experiment *(noun)* a test or trial to discover something unknown, or to test an idea.

stunt *(noun)* 1. an acrobatic, dangerous, or spectacular action; 2. anything spectacular or unusual done to gain publicity.

a **What does the word 'experiment' suggest about the writer's attitude to the event?**

b **What does the word 'stunt' suggest about the writer's attitude to the event?**

c **The writer uses the word 'experiment' only once, and the word 'stunt' twice. What does this suggest about the writer's point of view?**

2 **Look closely at paragraphs 7 and 8 in the article. Why do you think the writer has chosen to include evidence from research commissioned by the BBC?**

3 **Now that you have closely examined the language and evidence in the article, can you say any more about the writer's point of view?**

Activity 3 | Get ahead at GCSE

Your form teacher has given you the letter opposite from your head teacher to take home.

1 **What point do you think the school hopes this experiment will make?**

2 **If you were writing a newspaper report on this event, which of the following words would you use to get your point of view across?**

an experiment   a stunt   a race   research

3 **Which of the pieces of evidence on the right would you choose to help you get your point across – and in what order would you include them in your report?**

4 **Write a short newspaper report on the event.**

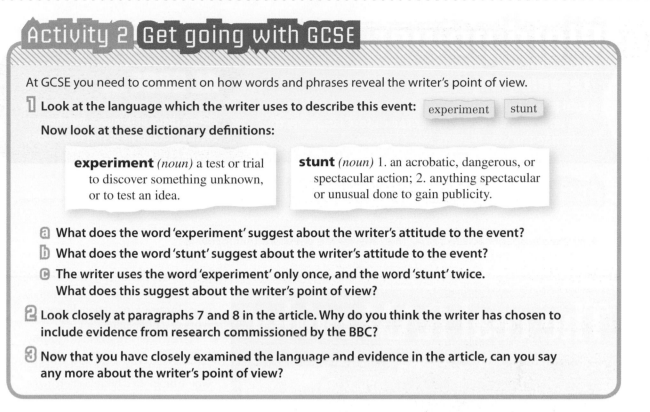

Dear Parents/Guardians

As you may know, next week is Green Week in school. We are particularly keen to encourage our students to walk to school during this week and your support would be greatly appreciated. As part of Green Week, the Science Department will be conducting an experiment in which one student will walk half a mile to school, while another will travel exactly the same distance by car.

'Walking to school is the healthy choice which we would encourage all students to make.' **Head teacher**

'Walking might be healthy but the area round the school is deadly. The roads are unsafe and the pollution is terrible. There's no way my boy is walking to school.' **A parent**

'A recent survey shows that only 35% of secondary school students are driven to school.' **A local councillor**

5 Word power

Learning objective

I am learning:
- to understand how a writer can choose language to change the way readers react to texts.

At GCSE ...

At GCSE you will need to comment on the writer's choice of language and choose effective vocabulary in your own writing.

Activity 1 Get ready for GCSE

Read the newspaper article below, then answer the questions that follow it.

The real RAM raider

1 When Ed and Paula Smith returned home after a pleasant stroll in the country, they were greeted by a scene of utter devastation.

2 An intruder had smashed through their patio doors and gone on a wrecking spree inside, causing at least £7,000 worth of damage.

3 The carpets and wallpaper in their £550,000 home were ruined, their range cooker had been smashed, their plasma television was wrecked and several items of furniture were badly damaged.

4 The horrified couple could only imagine it was the work of a burglar – or a gang of thugs with a grievance who had broken in to exact a terrible revenge.

5 In fact, the chaos had a rather more bizarre explanation. It was the work of a rampaging ram.

6 He had been in the field of a nearby farm when he managed to escape. He got into the Smiths' garden where he spotted his reflection in the patio doors.

7 Believing it to be another ram he charged the doors and smashed his way into the house.

8 Once inside he spotted a reflection of a ram in the door of the expensive range cooker and then in the shiny television screen and then in the polished furniture. Despite the best efforts of the pursuing farmer and his wife, the ram could not be controlled.

9 Mrs Smith, 50, said: 'We saw all the glass and all the mess and we were very scared. For about 15 minutes I was racking my brain wondering if I'd upset anyone for them to do this, while my husband was on the phone to the police reporting it.'

10 She added: 'I can understand now why they call them battering rams. The whole house stank because of the muck it left behind and I've had to throw out the rug in the living room. We are able to laugh about it though. Nobody has been hurt and everything can be replaced.'

Source: www.dailymail.co.uk

1 What did Mr and Mrs Smith think had happened when they returned from their walk?

2 What had actually happened – and why?

Activity 2 Get going with GCSE

At GCSE you will need to comment on why writers make particular language choices. You will also need to explain the effect of these choices.

1. The writer chose not to use the word 'ram' until the end of paragraph 5.
   a. What does the writer want the reader to think for the first four paragraphs?
   b. What effect does it have when she reveals that a ram caused the damage?

2. Look at some of the vocabulary the writer uses:

   devastation   smashed   wrecked

   a. Why do you think the writer has chosen this kind of vocabulary?
   b. Find **three** other examples of this kind of vocabulary. Try to explain the effect of using these words.

Results Plus
Top tip

When thinking about the effect of writers' vocabulary choices, it can be useful to think about what the effect would be if that particular word **wasn't** used.

Activity 3 Get ahead at GCSE

At GCSE you will need to choose your vocabulary carefully, thinking about its effect on the reader.

1. a. Imagine a ram broke into your school during lunchtime. You are going to write a short newspaper article describing what happened. What effect do you want your vocabulary choice to have on the reader?
   b. Now write some short paragraphs, describing:
   - what happened and why
   - the damage caused
   - how students and teachers reacted to the situation.

   Remember to choose your vocabulary carefully to create the effect you identified in question 1a.

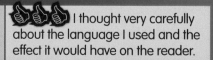

Results Plus
Assessment

The skill of selecting your vocabulary for effect will also help you succeed in your creative writing controlled assessment.

Assess yourself

Look at your answers to Activity 3. Use the table below to assess your work.

👍 I chose one or two words to help create the effect I wanted.	👍👍 I thought about the effect of some of the words I used.	👍👍👍 I thought very carefully about the language I used and the effect it would have on the reader.

Now look at the grade descriptions below. They show what you will need to do at GCSE.

Grade **F**	Grade **C**	Grade **A**
Students sometimes, but not always, choose their vocabulary for effect.	Students use a variety of vocabulary to create different effects and engage the reader.	Students use imaginative and ambitious vocabulary for a range of effects.

6 Explain yourself

Learning objective

I am learning:
• to develop my comments on a text in more detail.

At GCSE ...

At GCSE you will need to analyse texts in detail and depth.

Activity 1 Get ready for GCSE

Read the newspaper article below, then answer the questions that follow it.

VACUUM CLEANER-MAN!
Inventor uses suction to crawl up a wall, Spider-Man-style

1 **In the Spider-Man comics and movies, mild-mannered Peter Parker finds himself able to climb up the side of buildings after being bitten by a radioactive spider.**

2 In real life, enterprising scientist Jem Stansfield got the same effect from two vacuum cleaners he bought at Tesco.

3 He adapted the household appliances' motors into giant sucker pads, then used them to crawl up a 30ft wall.

4 A crowd of amazed onlookers watched the presenter from BBC One's *Bang Goes The Theory* scale the side of a school and retrieve a lost shuttlecock from the roof as part of the Brighton Science Festival Programme.

5 He completed the daredevil stunt without a safety helmet after fixing the cleaners to a back pack attached to two 'vacuum gloves'.

6 Afterwards Mr Stansfield, 39, an aeronautics graduate who weighs about 12st, said: 'I came across the idea when I was doing a challenge to make superhuman powers out of junk.

7 'I worked out the vacuum cleaners could support my weight.

8 'I attached pads roughly the size of tea trays to the nozzle and realised they pressed tightly against the wall and could hold me.'

9 Festival organiser Richard Robinson admitted he thought the stunt would flop when he was told about it.

10 He said: 'We all laughed. We didn't think it would ever work, then we turned around and he was climbing a wall.'

11 Before becoming a TV presenter, Mr Stansfield created special effects for films.

12 For his next trick, he hopes to drive a car all the way from London to Manchester, powered only by coffee beans.

Source: www.dailymail.co.uk

1 **Read the question opposite:** How does the writer suggest that Jem Stansfield's experiment is amazing and exciting?

a **Read the article again, writing down evidence that you could use to support your answer to the question above.**

b **Now sort your evidence into groups. For example, you could organise your evidence under these three headings (or you could choose your own):**
   • the opening of the article
   • the way the writer describes the materials Jem Stansfield used to climb the wall
   • the reactions of other people.

Activity 2 Get going with GCSE

Now you need to think about turning your points and your evidence into paragraphs. Look at this opening to a point-evidence-explanation paragraph:

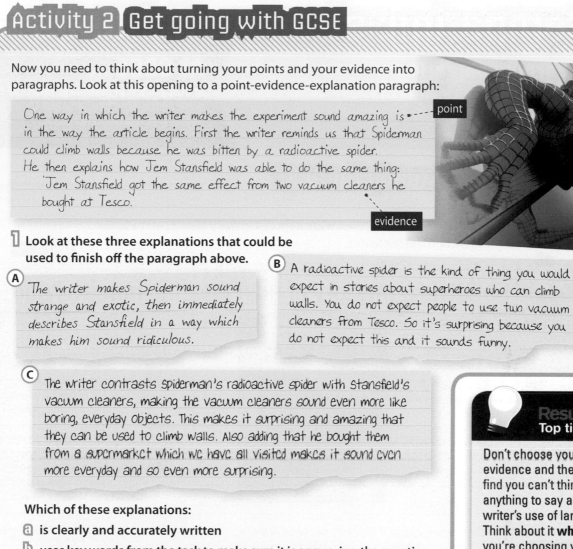

One way in which the writer makes the experiment sound amazing is — **point** in the way the article begins. First the writer reminds us that Spiderman could climb walls because he was bitten by a radioactive spider. He then explains how Jem Stansfield was able to do the same thing:
'Jem Stansfield got the same effect from two vacuum cleaners he bought at Tesco. — **evidence**

1 **Look at these three explanations that could be used to finish off the paragraph above.**

A The writer makes Spiderman sound strange and exotic, then immediately describes Stansfield in a way which makes him sound ridiculous.

B A radioactive spider is the kind of thing you would expect in stories about superheroes who can climb walls. You do not expect people to use two vacuum cleaners from Tesco. So it's surprising because you do not expect this and it sounds funny.

C The writer contrasts Spiderman's radioactive spider with Stansfield's vacuum cleaners, making the vacuum cleaners sound even more like boring, everyday objects. This makes it surprising and amazing that they can be used to climb walls. Also adding that he bought them from a supermarket which we have all visited makes it sound even more everyday and so even more surprising.

Which of these explanations:

ⓐ is clearly and accurately written

ⓑ uses key words from the task to make sure it is answering the question

ⓒ comments closely on the writer's choice of language

ⓓ is the best response?

Results**Plus**
Top tip

Don't choose your evidence and then find you can't think of anything to say about the writer's use of language. Think about it **while** you're choosing your evidence – and pick quotations about which you know you've got something interesting and relevant to say.

Activity 3 Get ahead at GCSE

Write **two** further point-evidence-explanation paragraphs answering the question:

How does the writer suggest that Jem Stansfield's experiment is amazing and exciting?

You can use the evidence you selected in Activity 1 and the examples above to help you. Remember, you should aim to:

● write clearly and accurately
● use key words from the task
● comment closely on the writer's choice of language.

Results**Plus**
Watch out!

Your explanation should not simply repeat your point. It should explain the effect that your evidence is meant to have on the reader, and how and why the writer achieved this.

7 Comparing: strange sightings

Learning objective

I am learning:
• to compare the structure, language and ideas in two related texts.

At GCSE ...

At GCSE you will be asked to compare the presentation, structure, language choice and ideas in two different texts.

Activity 1 Get ready for GCSE

Read the two newspaper articles below, then write a short summary of each of these two strange sightings in two or three sentences.

Text A

Google Streetview mystery of man wearing horse's head

1 **This is 'Horseboy', who has become an Internet sensation after being snapped by Google Streetview.**

2 The mystery man wearing a horse head mask ambushed the Google car as it uploaded street scenes on to the Internet. Now the search is on to uncover his identity.

3 IT manager Russell Moffatt, 50, saw the snap of Horseboy, taken on a quiet Aberdeen street in Hardgate, near Riverside Terrace, while searching for an optician.

4 Dad-of-one Russell said: 'It was really funny. He obviously spotted the Google car photographing streets, ran to get a horse head mask and laid in wait for it.'

5 The joker, wearing a purple jumper and black jeans, can be seen pulling on the realistic mask. But he is so far away from the camera that he cannot be recognised.

6 The picture joins a list of unusual sights caught on Streetview since its February launch – including two men wearing scuba gear and brandishing a harpoon chasing a Google car down a road in Norway.

Source: www.mirror.co.uk

Text B

Girl, 15, tells of terror after being stalked through forest by a big cat she claims was a PANTHER

1 A 15-year-old schoolgirl has told of her terror after being chased by a big cat she claims was a 'black panther' in the Forest of Dean, Gloucestershire.

2 Kim Howells was enjoying a walk through the woodland on her 15th birthday with her cousin Sophie Gwynne, eight, when they came across the animal lying beneath a tree.

3 Ms Howells, who described the 'panther' as about the size of a Great Dane dog, with big eyes, paws and a long tail, said the creature began following them after they spotted it at around 8.30pm on Monday night.

4 She said: 'We carried on walking but then I looked back and it was sitting up looking at me.

5 'It was definitely a big cat. I've seen wild boar and deer in the Forest before and it definitely wasn't one of them. What makes me sure is that it was still light so I could see it really clearly.'

6 Ms Howells added: 'Sophie was asking what it was and then we looked behind us and it was about five metres away, following us.

7 The pair then ran all the way back to Ms Howells's family home in nearby Ruspidge.

8 It is not the first time a big cat sighting has been reported near Ruspidge. In June 2007, milkman Robert Brinton got an early morning wake-up call when he encountered a big cat in Railway Road.

Source: www.dailymail.co.uk

Activity 2 Get going with GCSE

1 Can you make any connection between what these two articles are about?

2 Look at the structure of the two articles.

   a Are the opening paragraphs of the two articles similar in any way?

   b Are the final paragraphs of the two articles similar in any way?

3 Do you think the two writers want the reader to react in the same way to 'Horseboy' and the panther? Use a table like the one below to help you gather ideas:

	'Horseboy' article	Panther article
The writer describes the creature as …		
The writer describes witnesses' reactions …		
This is intended to make the reader feel …		
The writer's choice of the word …		
… suggests that …		

Activity 3 Get ahead at GCSE

At GCSE, for your controlled assessment you will be asked to compare two texts. Use this activity as a chance to practise this skill.

Using the ideas you collected in Activity 2, write a comparison of the two newspaper articles. Aim to compare:
- what they are about
- the structure of the two articles
- the writers' points of view and intended effects on the reader.

Look back at page 43 to remind yourself how to write effective point-evidence-explanation paragraphs.

You could use the paragraph openings below to help you:

The opening of the Horseboy article is …

Similarly, the opening of the Panther article …

At the end of the Horseboy article the writer is …

In the same way, at the end of the Panther article …

The writer's attitude in the Horseboy article is …

However, in the Panther article the writer seems to be …

ResultsPlus
Top tip

Always think about the effect each writer wants to have on the reader – but don't keep using the same word to describe it. Think of other words with similar meanings.

In this activity you are going to look at extracts from some sample answers to Activity 3 on page 45. An examiner has commented on the extracts and suggested a grade, but he has not shown which comment belongs to which answer.

Your task:
- Read the different student answer extracts.
- As you read, think about the strengths and weaknesses of the answers.
- Read the examiner's comments.
- Work out which comment belongs to which answer.

Like a real examiner, you could be asked to explain your choices so make sure you have reasons ready to support your answers.

Extract from student answer 1 Grade

> Both articles are about weird things that people have seen. One was a man with a horse mask and the other was a panther. One was on the Internet and the other one was in real life. The one on Google is funny. The one on the panther isn't so funny. I think it is meant to be scary but no-one knows for sure whether the panther is real or not – it might just be a cat or the whole thing could be a big joke. The chances of it being a real panther are small. I don't think they live around here. Maybe one escaped from a zoo or something.

Extract from student answer 2 Grade

> The biggest difference between the two articles is in the way the writer wants the reader to think and feel. In the Horse Boy article, we are not meant to take this strange sighting very seriously. The man who found the picture on the Internet describes it as 'really funny' and the writer describes the man in the mask as a 'joker'. Although it is not clear in the panther article whether the two girls really did see a big cat, we are told about the effect it has on them. The writer begins the article by describing the girls' 'terror' which makes you realise from the very start how scared you would be with a panther chasing you.

Extract from student answer 3 Grade

> The newspaper article about Horse Boy is meant to be funny. It tells you how a man found the picture of the man in the horse mask while he was on the Internet looking for an optician. It's also quite mysterious because no one knows who the man in the mask is. The other article about the panther is meant to make you feel scared for the two girls who were followed through the woods. You can tell the girls were scared because they ran all the way home.

This extract from the student's answer is typical of E grade performance. The student has made a comparison between the content of the two articles, recognising a connection between them and pointing out a difference. While there is some comment on the effect of one of the articles, there is little comparison made and the point is not developed with any evidence or explanation. Some of the comments on the panther article do not answer the question and so cannot contribute to the grade awarded. If the rest of the answer was of a similar standard, they would most likely achieve a grade E.

D **Examiner comment 2**

This extract from the student's answer is typical of D grade performance. The student notes a range of different effects which the two articles are intended to have on the reader but only makes a brief reference to one text to support this. There is no explanation of how the writer has achieved these different effects or reference to language choice. If the student sustained this level throughout their response, it is likely that they would achieve a grade D.

C **Examiner comment 3**

This extract from the student's answer is typical of C grade performance. The student effectively compares the effect of both articles on the reader. It uses a range of different evidence, selecting evidence from different parts of one article to support the comparison. There is some comment on one writer's choice of language, recognising the effect of its position in the text. If the student sustained this level in the rest of their response, they would most likely achieve a grade C.

1 Choose the weakest of the three student answer extracts on page 46. Use the relevant Examiner comment to annotate the student answer with suggestions on how to improve it.

2 Now look at your own answer to this activity. Compare it to the three extracts from student answers on page 46.
  • Which one is your answer closest to?
  • Discuss or jot down what you might need to do to improve your answer if you were to do it again.

8 Going solo

Learning objective

I am learning:
- to prepare and present a solo speaking and listening task.

At GCSE ...

At GCSE you will be assessed on your ability to communicate clearly.

At GCSE you could be asked to give a talk on a subject or topic. This will be assessed and will count towards your final grade.

Activity 1 Get ready for GCSE

Read the magazine article below, then answer the questions that follow it.

Strangedays GHOST WATCH

Inverary Castle Phantom

Visit Inverary Castle in Argyll, Scotland, and the welcoming guides will tell you stories of hauntings in the area, including a White Lady who appears on a nearby bridge and inside houses on the Inverary estate.
5 A ghostly galleon traditionally materialises above Loch Fyne as a death warning to the Dukes of Argyll and other family members.

Unusual incidents have also been reported within the castle itself, but perhaps the most remarkable is 10 the phantom harpist, whose music also acts as a death warning to the family. In 1949, the 10th Duke of Argyll was dying at the castle, attended by a doctor and a local minister. Suddenly, the sound of harp music was heard from an adjoining room. The doctor and minister both 15 left the bedside briefly to see who might be playing an instrument. On their return, the Duke had died.

According to the story most frequently told today (and included on the castle's own website) the **spectral** harpist is a young boy who was murdered in 1644, 20 during an attack on the castle led by James Graham, Marquis of Montrose. The website claims 'a young Irish boy of 12 or 13 employed to play the harp' was killed and dismembered, with his body parts thrown on the bed in the MacArthur Room. Thereafter, his ghost was 25 said to haunt the room.

Source: www.forteantimes.com

1 Write down all the details that the writer includes to make the story spooky and disturbing.

2 For each detail you find, write a sentence explaining how it adds to the mood of the article.
You could record your answers in a table like this:

Detail	Adds to the spooky mood because...
The ghost is not seen but is heard playing the harp. The harp music is a 'death warning'.	It's unusual for a ghost to play the harp – and harp music is quite spooky anyway.

Glossary

spectral: ghostly

Activity 2 Get going with GCSE

You are going to write a speech in which you tell your audience about a supernatural incident and then explain whether you believe in ghosts and why.

1 First, you need to write your description of a supernatural incident. You could plan it like this:

Where you were
- Place
- Time of day
- The weather
- What you were doing

The incident
- How did it start?
- And then?
- What did you see and hear?

How you felt
- Were you scared or intrigued?
- How did it feel?

What happened afterwards
- Did everything go back to normal?
- Or had something changed?

2 Now write your description, including lots of descriptive language to help your listeners picture the scene.

3 Next you need to write a paragraph telling your listeners:
- if you believe in ghosts or not
- how and why this supernatural incident made up your mind.

ResultsPlus
Watch out!

Don't be tempted just to read your speech aloud. You need to **deliver** it to your audience, making regular eye contact with them and using non-verbal gestures to help hold their interest.

Activity 3 Get ahead at GCSE

Now prepare to **deliver** your speech to an audience. To do this you need to make cue cards.

1 Compare the opening of this student's written speech with her first cue card.

> It was dark and cold, nearly midnight and pouring with rain but I was tucked up in bed listening to music. The wind was howling outside my window, rattling the glass.

- dark, cold, nearly midnight
- pouring
- tucked up
- wind howling, rattling glass

Use this example to help you put your speech onto cue cards.

2 Now you need to think about the non-verbal features you are going to use in order to make your speech effective. Look at the checklist opposite and decide which features you are going to use in your speech.

3 Now use your cue cards to deliver your speech.

Make eye contact with people. ☐

Don't just make eye contact with one person though - try to make everyone feel included. ☐

Vary the tone of your voice appropriately. This can give your speech more impact. ☐

Use non-verbal gestures. Don't just stand like a statue - use your hands to emphasise and dramatise your speech. ☐

Speak loud enough so that everyone can hear you! ☐

Don't be tempted just to read your speech from a script. Use your cue cards as prompts; this will let you focus on **delivering** your speech. ☐

9 Writing for different purposes

Learning objective

I am learning:
• to write for different purposes.

At GCSE ...

At GCSE you will need to be able to write for different purposes and match your writing to those purposes.

Activity 1 Get ready for GCSE

Read Text A, taken from an online shop.

Text A

CRITTER CRUISER HAMSTER EXERCISE WHEEL

| **Description** | **Customer review** |

- Can be set to work stationary or moving
- Fun design
- Size: 10cm (4") x 7cm (3")
- Colour may vary
- Suitable for hamsters, gerbils and mice.

Let your pet exercise in style with this fun car. Three different settings allow the wheel to work in a stationary position or drive the car.

Source: www.the-rabbit-hutch-shop.com

1 a Write down all the **information** which this web page gives you about the Critter Cruiser.

b Write down any phrases or sentences that **describe** the Critter Cruiser.

c Write down any phrases or sentences that try to **persuade** the reader to buy the Critter Cruiser.

2 Invent a new toy for a pet or for a child. Write the text for an online shop's website to sell your new toy. You should:
- use the same structure as Text A: bullet points and a short paragraph
- make it informative, descriptive and persuasive.

Activity 2 Get going with GCSE

Read Text B, taken from another online shop.

Text B

Paw power!

No, your eyes do not deceive you; this really is an exercise car for little furry friends. Simply pop your pet inside the integrated exercise wheel and watch in amazement as paw power propels the fabulously silly Critter Cruiser along the
5 floor. Pets will have an absolute blast.

As well as giving critters a good workout, owners won't have to worry about keeping tabs on their pet every time it needs a bit of a run around. After all you can't really miss a brightly coloured comedy vehicle with a gerbil behind the wheel. But if you think you might, simply set
10 the wheel to stationary mode so your pet can exercise without cruising around the house.

If you want to treat your pet to something special but reckon traditional hamster wheels and rubber balls are old hat, this racy vehicle is just the ticket. On your paws, get set, scurry!

Source: www.firebox.com

Activity 2 continued...

1. How much of Text B is intended to:

   a. **inform** the reader
   b. **describe** the item for sale
   c. **persuade** the reader to buy it.

2. The writer of Text B uses lots of different persuasive techniques:

   > **alliteration**: two or more words near each other beginning with the same sound
   > **direct address**: talking directly to the reader
   > **informal language**: slang or conversational words and phrases
   > **humour**: language, ideas or images to make the reader laugh.

   Look at the quotations below. They are all taken from Text B. Which quotations are good examples of the four techniques listed above?

   No, your eyes do not deceive you

   furry friends

   paw power propels the fabulously silly Critter Cruiser

   Pets will have an absolute blast.

   a brightly coloured comedy vehicle with a gerbil behind the wheel

   traditional hamster wheels and rubber balls are old hat

   On your paws, get set, scurry!

3. What effect do each of these four techniques have on the reader? Look at some GCSE students' ideas below. Match them with the techniques and quotations you chose in question 2.

   gives the language emphasis

   makes the language sound punchy, powerful and fun

   makes you think it will be fun for the hamster and for you

   makes you feel like the writer is talking to you

   you enjoy reading the advert, you think you will enjoy owning the product

   suggests that this is someone you know and can trust

4. Which of the ideas above should you avoid using because it doesn't really mean anything?

Activity 3 Get ahead at GCSE

Ar GCSE, the best writing uses techniques that help achieve the purpose of the writing. Practise this now.

1. Look again at the informative, descriptive and persuasive text that you wrote in Activity 1 question 2.

   a. Rewrite it, trying to make it as persuasive as Text B.
   b. Try to use the four persuasive techniques you explored in Activity 2.

2. Circle or underline examples of **each** of these four persuasive techniques in your writing. If there are any you have forgotten to include, try to add them in.

ResultsPlus Top tip

Plan your writing before you start. What are the three or four key points you will use to persuade your audience?

ResultsPlus Assessment

Using techniques for effect is something that will help you succeed in your controlled assessment writing as well as in your exams.

10 From start to finish

learning objective

I am learning:
• to structure my writing so it has the most impact.

At GCSE ...

At GCSE you need to understand how writers structure their texts – and demonstrate that you can effectively structure your own writing.

Activity 1 Get ready for GCSE

Read the article below, then answer the questions on page 51.

Features: Articles

All Fall Down

1 The morning of 13 July 1980 was a fresh one, promising a glorious summer Sunday for the annual Hollinwell Show in the small town of Kirkby-in-Ashfield. The highlight would be a competition involving around 500 children in 11 junior marching bands, for which they had all been practising their music and routines for months. No one could have guessed that this would become, in a policeman's words, 'like a battlefield with bodies everywhere'.

2 Most children had got up especially early and were brought by coaches from as far as 65km away. They arrived tired, restless and certainly nervous for the nine o'clock start. It promised to be a long day, and it began with a long wait as the judges made their final inspection. There was no more time for rehearsals, only for last-minute checks.

3 Just after 10:30, the children and some adults began collapsing. They were ferried by dozens of ambulances to four local hospitals, where about 259 children were examined and nine were detained overnight. Symptoms included fainting, running eyes, sore throats, dizziness, vomiting, trembling,

weakness, numbness and a metallic taste in the mouth… but neither all at once nor all felt by the same person.

4 An organiser for one of the bands, Terry Bingham, said: 'We were ready for the display when one or two children collapsed. Then a few more went, and a few more. We called off the event but others fell as they came out of the arena. Then spectators started dropping.'

5 One of the girls affected, Petula Merriman, 14, said: 'We were on the field in full uniform for an inspection… I've never had to stand to attention that long before. As we marched off, I tried to grab hold of my drum but just fell on the floor. My friends were collapsing all around me.'

6 The first thought of many of those standing around the arena staring in disbelief at the numbers of children keeling over, was 'food poisoning'. It became clear this theory was not tenable; many of the children had only consumed supplies which they had brought with them in their coaches.

7 Some people believed they saw a cloud of insecticide drifting across the showground; others speculated about the dust raised by the feet of several hundred marchers.

This seemed to be confirmed by a spokesman at the Queens Medical Centre, Nottingham, who said that the children taken there had symptoms 'consistent with exposure to fumes of some kind'. Police tracked down the farmer who owned the adjacent field: it had not been sprayed for more than 10 years.

8 Having eliminated the improbable, the authorities edged towards the unthinkable. At an evening press briefing, Chief Inspector Ogden admitted: 'The whole thing is a complete mystery. A gymkhana was held in the same field later without trouble.'

1 Look at the first five paragraphs of the article again. Write a very short summary of the events at Hollinwell.

2 a Make a list of all the different possible explanations mentioned in the article.

b Which explanation do you think is the most believable? Write a sentence or two explaining why.

Dr John Wood, director of health for the Kirkby area, added that he was becoming convinced that 'mass hysteria' was, indeed, the only possibility, since tests had 'virtually eliminated the alternatives'.

9 These findings (or lack of them) were greeted with scorn by offended parents and show organisers. '[They] are rubbish', fumed Terry Bingham. 'There has been a cover-up. Some people are still feeling ill, so how can it have been hysteria?' Viewer reaction to a BBC TV documentary made 23 years later included such comments as 'Mass hysteria is a way of covering up the truth'; 'No one will ever convince me that just one child fainting could cause over 200 to come down with those symptoms'.

10 Although we know more about the Hollinwell collapse now, none of it has resolved the matter conclusively. The pro- and anti-hysteria camps are *still* as far apart as ever.

Source: www.forteantimes.com

Activity 2 Get going with GCSE

At GCSE you will need to think about how to write effective openings. You can learn a lot from how other writers do this.

1 Look again at the opening paragraph of the article.

a Why has the writer begun by using the adjectives 'fresh' and 'glorious'?

b Why has the writer finished this first paragraph with the policeman's quote comparing the scene to a 'battlefield'?

c The opening paragraph does not explain **why** the show looked like a battlefield. Why do you think the writer has withheld this information?

2 Now look at the second paragraph.

a Make a list of all the details that the writer includes about the children and their mood.

b What effect does all this detail have?

3 The writer could have begun the story in lots of different ways. For example:

Opening 1

In 1980, at the Hollinwell Show, hundreds of adults and children mysteriously collapsed and were hospitalised.

Opening 2

Hundreds of visitors to the Hollinwell Show in 1980 came expecting to see a marching band competition. Nothing could have prepared them for the horror they were about to witness.

Opening 3

Was it food poisoning? A cloud of poisonous gas? Or just hysteria? Why did hundreds of children collapse at the Hollinwell Show?

a Which alternative opening do you think is the most effective?

b Write a sentence or two explaining your choice.

Activity 3 Get ahead at GCSE

Writers use lots of different techniques for openings and endings. For example:

a set the scene with lots of engaging description

b hook the reader's attention with a dramatic event

c intrigue the reader

d explain how it all ended

e summarise what happened

f bring the reader up to date with the most recent information

g leave the reader wondering what happened next

h a surprising twist the reader wasn't expecting

i introduce the main characters involved

1 **Sort these techniques into ones which would work well in the openings and endings of:**
   - fiction (a short story, for example)
   - non-fiction (such as a magazine article)
   - neither.

   You could use a table like the one below to help.

	Openings	Endings
Fiction		
Non-fiction		
Neither		

2 **You have been asked to write a magazine article about a mysterious but true incident. Choose one of the three ideas on these pages, or make up an incident of your own.**

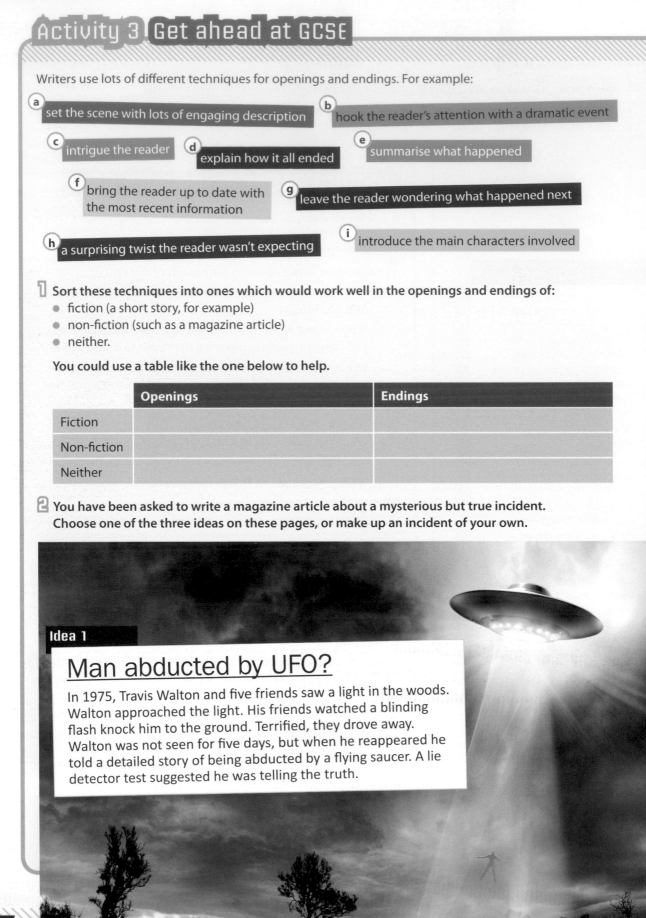

Idea 1

Man abducted by UFO?

In 1975, Travis Walton and five friends saw a light in the woods. Walton approached the light. His friends watched a blinding flash knock him to the ground. Terrified, they drove away. Walton was not seen for five days, but when he reappeared he told a detailed story of being abducted by a flying saucer. A lie detector test suggested he was telling the truth.

Idea 2

Thunder fish strike London

London was hit by a vast thunderstorm in May 1984. A man in West Ham was surprised at the noise of the rain on his roof – but even more surprised when he went out the next morning to find hundreds of small fish on his roof and on the pavement.

Idea 3

Casper the charitable ghost

A garage in Doncaster was haunted by a mischievous ghost who threw coins at the staff and customers. Owner, Nigel Lee, collected the coins but never found an explanation. When the haunting stopped after a number of months, Mr Lee had collected more than £7 in small change.

Results Plus
Top tip

Don't make your opening too mysterious. If the reader can't work out what's going on, they won't be hooked and they might stop reading.

3 Look at your answer to question 1. Using one or more of the techniques that you decided were effective for non-fiction openings, write the **first** paragraph of your article.

4 Look again at your answer to question 1. Using one or more of the techniques that you decided were effective for non-fiction endings, write the **final** paragraph of your article.

Assess yourself

Look at your answers to questions 3 and 4 of Activity 3, above. Use the table below to assess your work.

👍 I wrote an opening and an ending about the mysterious incident.	👍👍 I tried to use techniques in my opening and ending for a particular effect.	👍👍👍 I carefully chose ideas and language for effect in my opening and in my ending.

Now look at the grade descriptions below. They show what you will need to do at GCSE.

Grade **F**	Grade **C**	Grade **A**
Students use some techniques and vocabulary to interest the reader.	Students successfully use techniques and a variety of vocabulary to engage the reader.	Students use techniques and vocabulary creatively to engage and hold the reader's interest.

11 Striking sentences

Learning objective

I am learning:
• to vary the length of my sentences for effect.

At GCSE ...

At GCSE you will need to use a variety of carefully crafted sentences to create a range of effects.

Activity 1 Get ready for GCSE

Read the newspaper article below, then answer the question that follows it.

School stops ball games after noise complaints from neighbours

1 Children at a Selby school have had their daily afternoon break cancelled and been banned from playing ball at other playtimes because neighbours have complained they are too noisy.

2 Barlby Community Primary School, in Hill Top, has been on the site for 100 years, but three neighbours in Acorn Close have complained to Selby District Council about the noise the 350 children make at playtimes. Football has now been banned in the playground and the afternoon break cancelled. The complaints have been met with disgust by local councillor Brian Marshall.

3 He said: 'I am fuming. There has been a school on that site for more than 100 years. Why did they buy a house next to a school? For young children to be out playing and laughing, there is nothing nicer. The governors should do nothing and let the children play.'

4 But one resident, who refused to say whether he had complained or not, said the old school had been demolished and then rebuilt, which now meant the noise was channelled through the houses adjoining the playground. It was also suggested that another complaint had been made because an estate agent had told the householder the noise devalued the house.

5 In a letter to parents, Alistair McCloud, chairman of the governors, said the school refuted all suggestions there was a problem with noise. But in an attempt to be a good neighbour, the school had arranged for an acoustic fence to be put up.

6 However, this did not satisfy the complainers and the moans continued. An offer to erect a further fence this year was rejected by the neighbours, who instead asked that the children's fun be curtailed.

7 Break times are now staggered so fewer children are in the playground at any one time.

8 Elaine Spooner, who lives in Acorn Close, said she had grandchildren and godchildren at the school. She said: 'The children are at school, what do you want them to do? I think the people who have complained are small-minded. There's nothing as nice as hearing kids play. It's not as if it's a senior school where you might get bad language.'

Source: www.yorkpress.co.uk

Imagine you are a student at this school. Send a text to a friend, explaining what has happened giving as much detail as you can. Remember, you must write your text message using no more than 140 characters.

Activity 2 Get going with GCSE

At GCSE you will need to comment on how writers vary sentence length for effect. You will also need to vary the length of sentences in your own writing.

1 Write down the first word of each sentence in the article. How many words are used more than once?

2 Varying the openings of your sentences is a really good way to create sentence variety in your writing. Look at this sentence:

> Break times are now staggered so fewer children are in the playground at any one time.

This sentence could be re-written in lots of different ways:

> Now break times are staggered so fewer children are in the playground at any one time.

> So that fewer children are in the playground at any one time, break times are now staggered.

> The school has decided to stagger break times so fewer children are in the playground at any one time.

Re-write the sentence opposite in as many different ways as you can:

> In a letter to parents, Alistair McCloud, chairman of the governors, said the school refuted all suggestions there was a problem with noise.

Activity 3 Get ahead at GCSE

1 Look at the quotations in the article: one from the councillor, Brian Marshall, and one from a neighbour, Elaine Spooner.

a What do you notice about the length of the sentences that the writer has used here?

b What does this sentence length suggest about the kind of voice in which these two people were speaking?

> Barlby Community Primary School, in Hill Top, has been on the site for 100 years, but three neighbours in Acorn Close have complained to Selby District Council about the noise the 350 children make at playtimes. Football has now been banned in the playground and the afternoon break cancelled.

2 Look at the two sentences opposite from paragraph 2 in the article:

a The second sentence is much shorter than the first. What effect does this have?

b Imagine you are a neighbour of this school and are writing a letter to complain about the noise. Write the first two sentences of your letter: use a long sentence to explain the situation, then add a short sentence giving your opinion of it.

3 Now imagine you are the head teacher of the school, writing a letter in reply to this neighbour. Write two or three paragraphs explaining what you have done and how you feel about the situation. Aim to:
- use a variety of first words in your sentences
- use some short sentences for impact
- use some longer sentences followed by shorter sentences for even greater impact.

ResultsPlus Top tip

Every time you complete a longer piece of writing, do a quick survey of your sentences. Have you used a variety of first words? Are your sentences a variety of lengths? If not, look for sentences where a quick re-write will create variety.

12 Putting it all together

learning objective

I am learning:
• to use all the skills I have developed in this unit to complete a GCSE-style writing task.

At GCSE ...

At GCSE your writing is assessed for the range of skills you have been practising in this unit.

Activity 1 Get ready for GCSE

You are going to complete this GCSE-style writing task:

Write an article for your local newspaper about something surprising or amazing that has happened in your area.

Think about the kind of incident which you could use for your article. You could choose from one of the options below:

an animal behaving in a surprising way, like the ram who vandalised a house

something mysterious and unexplained, like the Hollinwell Show

an unusual tourist attraction, like Inverary Castle

an amazing stunt, like someone climbing a building using two vacuum cleaners

a shocking decision made by a local school, like the banning of ball games at Barlby Primary School

something else

Write a summary of what your newspaper article will be about in just one sentence.

Activity 2 Get going with GCSE

At GCSE the best writing is planned writing. Planning helps you organise your ideas and structure your writing for effect.

1 **Look at the summary which you wrote in Activity 1. Create a spider diagram like the one opposite, listing any questions you need to think about before you start writing.**

2 **What will be your perspective or point of view in the article? Will you treat it as a funny story? A serious story? Write a sentence or two explaining your decision.**

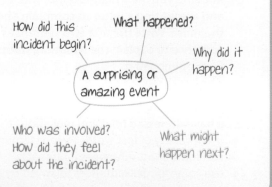

How did this incident begin?

What happened?

Why did it happen?

A surprising or amazing event

Who was involved? How did they feel about the incident?

What might happen next?

Activity 2 continued...

3 Think about your opening paragraph. To help you, look at the opening paragraphs of the newspaper articles on pages 40, 42 and 44.

　a Write a sentence about each article, explaining the kind of opening the writer has used.

　b What kind of opening will you use for your article? You could make a table like the one below to help you plan your ideas.

Paragraph	Plan
1	Opening: summarise story in a sentence or two
2	
6	
7	Ending:

4 How will you end your article? Look at the same newspaper articles on pages 40, 42 and 44.

　a Write a sentence about each article, explaining the kind of ending the writer has used.

　b What kind of ending will you use? Add your idea to your planning table.

5 Now think about the middle paragraphs of your article.

　a What extra details and information will you include?

　b Think about the people involved in the incident and what they might say about it. Which of their quotations will you use?

　c Now decide in which paragraphs you will use these details and quotations. Add them to your planning table.

Activity 3 Get ahead at GCSE

1 Now write your newspaper article. Remember to:

- give your article a headline
- think carefully about your choice of detail, language and quotation, making sure they support your chosen point of view and the effect you want to create
- use a variety of sentences and sentence lengths for effect.

2 When you have finished writing, check your work for:

- effective vocabulary choices
- sentence variety
- sense (is your meaning clear?)
- punctuation
- spelling.

ResultsPlus
Watch out!

If you're writing in an exam, don't skip planning your article and rush into writing it. Planning is the best way to make sure you have the best ideas in the best order.

In this activity you are going to look at some extracts from sample answers to Activity 3 on page 59. An examiner has commented on the extracts and suggested a grade, but he has not shown which comment belongs to which extract.

Your task:
- Read the different student answer extracts.
- As you read, think about the strengths and weaknesses of the answers.
- Read the examiner's comments.
- Work out which comment belongs to which answer.

Like a real examiner, you could be asked to explain your choices so make sure you have reasons ready to support your answers.

Extract from student answer 1   Grade

> The sun was shining and the hotel was very busy. The hotel was full of guests and they were about to eat their lunch in the dining room. The guests could not believe it when food started falling from the cieling and landing on their plates. The only thing was that the food was raw.
>
> 'I ordered fish but I wanted it cooked first,' said one of the guests. 'And I wanted chips with it but there weren't any.'

Extract from student answer 2   Grade

> It is thought to be the largest cheese sculpture ever made. Cheese sculpter, Bert Camen, said, 'It's an honour to have been asked to make it. There were times when I thought it would never be finished. But now I feel really proud. It looks magnificent.'
>
> The mayor said, 'This is something the whole town should be proud of. We're really putting ourselves on the map.'
>
> The sculpture which weights over 300 kilograms will be on display in the town hall until Thursday.

Extract from student answer 3   Grade (?)

> A horse escaped from a feild and ran down the high street. The horse was scaired and made loads of noise. The horse nocked over two poeple shopping. The horse made cars crash into each other because they were trying not to hit it and some people were hurt.

E Examiner comment 1

This extract from the student's answer is typical of E grade performance. The student has selected some good ideas and effectively ordered them. However, the choice of vocabulary is limited and the sentence structures are repetitive, frequently beginning with the same words. If the student sustained this type of writing throughout their response, they would probably achieve a grade E.

D Examiner comment 2

This extract from the student's answer is typical of D grade performance. The student has engaged the reader with a descriptive opening, withholding some information to build suspense. The answer is well paragraphed and spelling is generally accurate. Language choices are appropriate, but limited, but there is some variety in sentence structure. If the student sustained this type of writing throughout their response, they would probably achieve a grade D. A closer focus on these two areas would help lift this from a D grade towards a C grade.

C Examiner comment 3

This extract from the student's answer is typical of C grade performance. The student is beginning to use a wide variety of sentence types and structures with some effective vocabulary choices. Ideas are selected and developed well using quotations. The writing is accurately paragraphed and punctuated with only one or two spelling errors in more complex words. If the student sustained this level throughout their response, it is likely that they would achieve a grade C.

---

1 Choose the weakest student answer extract.
  a Re-write the extract so that it is more effective.
  b Annotate the changes you made, showing the student how you have improved their answer.

2 Now look at your own answer to this activity. Compare it to the three student answers on page 60.
  • Which one is your answer closest to?
  • Discuss or jot down what you might need to do to improve your answer if you were to do it again.

Unit 3
The Language Of Teenagers

How we talk and what we say is a huge part of our daily life but one that you might not have really thought about studying… until now!

Your spoken language literally says something about who you are. The words you use, the way in which you pronounce them, and the way you listen to and respond to others all affect how people perceive you, and the kind of impression and impact you make on others.

It's highly unlikely that you always use the same kind of talk though, and in this unit you will get the chance to explore how your own and others' spoken language changes and why this is. For example, it's unlikely you would use the same style of spoken language in all of the different scenarios below:

> You are talking to a friend about an amusing incident that happened at school.

> You are giving directions to a school visitor.

> You are giving a presentation or speech to an audience of parents and teachers, trying to persuade them about something.

> You are giving a presentation to your classmates about a cause or issue you feel passionate about.

> You are attending your first job interview.

> You have a Saturday job in a shop, and you are answering a customer's query.

In this unit you will explore how and why your spoken language changes. You will also experiment with writing for the spoken voice – for example, writing texts such as a script for a soap opera and a TV advert.

What am I learning in this unit?

In this unit you will start to develop some of the following skills that you will need at GCSE.

I will learn:
- what the difference is between spontaneous and scripted language.
- how my language changes depending on who I am talking to and why I am talking to them.
- what is meant by 'dialect' and 'slang'.
- how I use dialect and slang.
- what attitudes people have to different dialects and accents.
- what the features of spoken language are.
- what a transcript is and how to make one myself.
- how to collect and analyse my own spoken language data.
- some of the ways in which scripted language is made to sound like real spoken language.
- to write texts for the spoken voice.

Why do I need to know this?

If you take GCSE English Language there is a unit of work that focuses on analysing spoken language. As part of the unit you will need to demonstrate all of the skills listed above as part of two pieces of controlled assessment. The lessons in this unit are designed to focus specifically on the skills you will be assessed on when you start GCSE English Language. By practising and developing these skills now you can give yourself a head start so that when you do start GCSE you are prepared and ready to succeed!

1 Let's talk

Learning objective

I am learning:
- to identify the features of spoken and scripted language.

At GCSE ...

At GCSE you will need to identify the features of spoken language in order to comment on them.

Like most people you probably do a lot of talking! Just think about how many conversations you have had today. This kind of talk is called **spoken language**. Another term to describe spoken language is spontaneous language. It's likely you have also read and written play scripts over the last few years. Play scripts are examples of **scripted speech**. They **represent** spoken language – they are not the same as spoken language.

Activity 1 Get ready for GCSE

Look at the examples of language below.

a Yeah. Well. Maybe. No, don't think so.

b Hello Mum. Have you had a good day?

c Wadya want?

d What do you want? I do not like the look on your face.

e David: (whispers) Can you see them? They are over there near that tree.

f Alright? Er, how's it going?

g Um … Tuesday … or Wednesday.

h I'm not sure but I don't think that I will be going. It will be rather tedious.

1 a Which of them are most likely to be examples of spontaneous spoken language?

b Which are most likely to be examples of scripted spoken language? When you are doing this it might help to ask yourself whether you would ever talk in this way.

2 Copy and complete the table below, placing each of the examples into the correct column.

Spoken language	Scripted language

ResultsPlus
Watch out!

It's not always easy to work out whether examples of spoken language are real or scripted. Some writers are very talented at making their scripted language sound like real spoken language.

Activity 2 Get going with GCSE

Some of the examples in Activity 1 might have been difficult to put in the correct column. This is because some examples of scripted language are good at sounding just like spoken language.

1 **Which examples did you find easiest to place in the correct column? Make a list of these.**

2 **Now look at your list. For each example, write down what made it easy to decide whether it was an example of spoken or scripted language.**

3 **Now choose one example of spoken language and one example of scripted language. What are the main differences between the two? Think about:**
- how formal or informal the examples are
- which example includes hesitations and pauses
- whether you would speak in this way.

Activity 3 Get ahead at GCSE

At GCSE you will need to show you understand the features of spoken language.

1 **Read the example of a play script opposite in which two teenagers are talking.**

2 **Do you think the conversation sounds realistic all the way through?**

3 **Re-write the play script so that it sounds more like spontaneous spoken language. Think about adding some of the following:**
- pauses
- slang such as *newbie*
- hesitations such as *erm*, *uh*, etc.
- abbreviated words such as *don't* and *can't*.

4 **Ask two other people in your class to read your script out and judge how realistic it is on a scale of 1 to 10 (1 being not very realistic; 10 being very realistic).**

5 **Annotate your extract to explain what you have changed and why you have changed it. For example:**

> I changed 'Oh yes' to 'yeah'. I did this because 'Oh yes' sounded a bit too formal and not the kind of response a teenager would give to their friend.

Esther:	I went to Maths today.
David:	Oh yes.
Esther:	You know, with the new teacher.
David:	Of course.
Esther:	I went to sit in my usual seat and she shouted out, 'Where do you think you are going?'
David:	What did you say?
Esther:	Nothing. I was too shocked. I looked around and she was staring at me. She said, 'I have a seating plan. Who are you?'
David:	What did you do?
Esther:	I replied, quite calmly, 'And who are you?'
David:	You did! What did she say?
Esther:	She looked me in the eye and said, 'I am your teacher. And you are in detention.'

2 Don't talk to me like that!

learning objective

I am learning:
- how my language changes depending on who I am speaking to and why I am speaking to them.

At GCSE ...

At GCSE you will need to explore how spoken language changes according to purpose and audience.

Your spoken language will change depending on:
- the situation you are in (for example, your language may differ when you are talking as a student to a teacher to when you are a student talking to a friend)
- who you are talking to (your audience)
- why you are talking to them (the purpose).

One of the ways in which your language might change is in how **formal** or **informal** it becomes.

Formal language is the language used by newsreaders, or language you would use when being polite or talking to someone you do not know.

Informal language is the language that you would use among friends or at home.

Activity 1 Get ready for GCSE

1 a Read the sentences in the box below.

- Wanna go with us?
- Do you have the time please?
- *Valentine Weekend* are brill! I wanna see em live.
- Wassup?
- Nice one mate see ya later then.

- Sit down and listen carefully.
- The weather is inclement for this time of year.
- I love your hair. Where'd you get it done?
- Make sure your bedroom is tidy and all of your clothes have been put away.

b Place each of the sentences into the correct column in the table to show whether they are formal or informal language.

c In the final column, suggest who the speaker might be talking to. An example has been done for you.

Formal	Informal	Possible situation
Do you have the time please?		Asking someone for the time who you don't know very well or at all.

Activity 2 Get going with GCSE

A student is rehearsing a speech to be given to the school council, arguing that school uniform is unnecessary.

1 Read the opening paragraph of the student's speech opposite. Have they got the formality right?

2 The student has received some feedback from her teacher about the speech and it's not good news.

> Danielle,
> Thanks for trying but this isn't really acceptable. You need to pay more attention to what I've told you in class about getting the formality right. The council won't be impressed or persuaded by this. Needs further work.

> Hi. I wanna tell you why school uniform is rubbish. I hate it. Everyone does. What's with all the black eh? Black trousers, black blazer. I'm surprised we ain't got to wear black shirts an' all. And it's all uncomfortable innit. You know, we 'ave to do our top button up. Now that's uncomfortable. And it looks well stupid.

Your job is to advise Danielle on how to improve her work.

a Annotate the speech to show two or three examples where she is being too informal.

b Re-write the extract from Danielle's speech so that it is more suitable.

Activity 3 Get ahead at GCSE

At GCSE you will need to show you understand how spoken language changes according to context.

1 a Look at the different scenarios below.

b Choose two or three different scenarios and role-play how the conversation might sound. Remember to think about the situation, the audience and the purpose of the talk.

You are telling a friend about something amusing that happened in the previous lesson.

You are attending your first job interview.

You are a football manager talking to an angry press after a World Cup defeat.

Two school friends are having an argument.

One school friend is trying to persuade another to change their mind about something.

2 Write a short paragraph about how the language changed from one scenario to the next and why you think this is. Try to give specific examples. For example:

> When I was role-playing the interview, my language was formal because I wanted to make a good first impression and sound intelligent so that I got the job. For example, I started the interview by saying 'Good morning' and I told them I was 'a motivated, enthusiastic and hard-working person'. When I was role-playing me telling a friend about something amusing, my language was different because ...

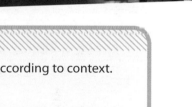

ResultsPlus
Watch out!

Informal language should not be thought of as 'worse' than formal language. The important thing is to choose the right level of formality for the purpose and audience of your talk. Sometimes your talk might need to move from formal to informal language, or the other way round.

3 What did they say?

learning objective

I am learning:
• what dialect and slang are and how they are used.

At GCSE ...

When analysing spoken language at GCSE you will need to consider how and why speakers' non-standard usage of language such as dialect and slang changes.

Slang refers to the informal words that are used by a social group. These words would be considered to be **non-standard vocabulary**. Slang changes very quickly.

Dialect refers to the words and grammar that are used in a particular area of the country. The words and grammar of dialect would be considered to be **non-standard English**.

Here are some examples of dialect and slang. Do you recognise any of them?

I'm wearing my daps tomorrow.

Happen she were unhappy.

Cool

Sick

Examples of dialect

Examples of slang

Come on, Bob, let's knock a blairze on an' we'll het

How bisti?

Mint

Grub

Activity 1 Get ready for GCSE

Some poets write in a particular dialect.

1 Read this extract from a poem written in Black Country dialect.

2 You've been asked to translate this poem into Standard English. Write the extract out using Standard English. If there are any words in dialect that you have not come across before, try and guess what they might mean.

Gerrit Darn Ya

My gran was allis brilliant
In everythin' 'er did
'N' 'er 'elped 't' rear me
When I was a kid

'Erd allis gorrer pinner on
Scrubbin' – Weshin' – Moppin flooers
'N' everywhere wuz spick 'n' span
When yow walked in the dooer

Activity 2 Get going with GCSE!

Now it's time to think about your own slang and dialect.

1. Make a list of dialect words for the area in which you live. You could start with dialect words for: ugly, attractive, unhappy, angry, frightened, sad, awkward.

2. Your school has been approached by a parents group who are concerned about not being able to understand what their sons and daughters are saying to them. They have sent you the email opposite:

   Start creating your dictionary of teenage slang. You could use the following layout:

   sick
   (adjective) Very good.
   Example: 'The movie was so sick.'

   Dear Teenagers,

   We need your help to create a dictionary of teenage language so we can understand what on earth you are saying!

   Please help us by:

   1 Making a list of the dialect and slang words you most often use.

   2 Writing a definition showing what the word means.

   3 Writing a sentence showing how you would use each word.

   Best wishes,
   Parents United

Activity 3 Get ahead at GCSE!

At GCSE you will need to think about why people might use informal language such as slang in some contexts, but not in others.

1. Choose **two** or more entries from your dictionary. Write down **one** situation in which it might be appropriate to use this piece of slang and **one** in which it would be inappropriate.

2. What makes the use of slang and dialect appropriate in some contexts but not others? Write a sentence or two explaining this. For example:

   The word 'sick' is something that my age group uses commonly, so my friend understands it. My gran wouldn't understand what I mean though, so I would need to change my language.

Assess yourself

Look back at your answer to Activity 3, question 2. Use the table below to assess your work.

👍 I know my language changes but can't always explain why this is.	👍👍 I gave a clear explanation of how my use of language changes.	👍👍👍 I explained confidently how my use of language changes.

Now look at the grade descriptions below. They show what you will need to do at GCSE.

Grade **F**	Grade **C**	Grade **A**
Students show some awareness of how they use spoken language.	Students explain and evaluate how they use spoken language.	Students explain in detail and give a persuasive evaluation of how they use spoken language.

4 First impressions

learning objective

I am learning:
- about attitudes towards features of spoken language such as accent and dialect.

At GCSE ...

At GCSE you need to explore people's attitudes to spoken language varieties.

We make judgements about people all the time. These can be based on the way someone looks or how they behave. Snap judgements can also be based on how a person speaks. This includes the vocabulary they use (such as dialect and slang) but also the way they pronounce words (their accent).

Activity 1 Get ready for GCSE

Look at the pieces of talk opposite:

1 **What snap judgements might you make about each of these people? For each person, write down:**
- how old you think they are
- how intelligent you think they are
- what kind of background they might be from.

2 **For each person, explain how you arrived at your views. For example:**

> I think person E is someone who sends lots of text messages because they use the word 'LOL' which is a term usually used in texts.

(a) I say, young man, demonstrate some consideration for others.

(b) 'e says, 'rubbish' so I says, I says, 'oi who'd yu think you're talkin' to?'

(c) Sometimes he con be a bit saft in 'is yed!

(d) Dang I if there ain't a gurt tra'er by 'er.

(e) And then he fell down the stairs. LOL.

(f) The glottal stop functions as a phoneme and can be appropriately transcribed.

3 **Share your judgements with other students in the class. Do they have similar views to you?**

Activity 2 Get going with GCSE

At GCSE you will need to show awareness of what other people think about varieties of spoken language such as accents.

Read the newspaper article on page 71 then answer these questions.

1 **Some people apply stereotypes to certain accents. For example, people speaking in a particular type of Yorkshire accent are often seen as very trustworthy and honest.**
   (a) **Make a list of any regional accents you are aware of.**
   (b) **Do you apply any stereotypes, good or bad, to these accents?**

Activity 2 continued...

2 Do you think stereotypes should be taken seriously? For example, do you think every single person from Yorkshire is 100% trustworthy? Or that people with certain accents are 'thick'? Write a paragraph explaining your reasons.

3 Now think about your own accent. Do you think people make judgements about you based on your accent?

4 Read the article again. Who do you agree with more: Beryl Bainbridge or Professor Michael Tooley? Explain your reasons.

Wednesday 29 January 2009

Wipe-out regional accents

1 Last night, novelist Beryl Bainbridge argued that regional accents should be wiped out. She claimed that children should have compulsory elocution lessons so that they learn how to pronounce words correctly.

2 She might have a point. Research has shown that employers think that people with certain accents sound less intelligent, whatever they say. On the other hand, people who have softly spoken Scottish accents are trusted by employers.

3 However, Professor Michael Tooley of Birmingham University is a big supporter of regional accents. He says that getting rid of regional accents would produce a 'sterile and poorer culture.' Clive Upton of Leeds University goes further when he argues that 'What we say is who we are. We are talking about our identities when we talk about our accents.'

4 Television seems to be playing its part in protecting regional accents. Presenters such as Adrian Chiles and Huw Edwards speak in their regional accents with pride.

Activity 3 Get ahead at GCSE

Your school has been asked to join a national debate on whether regional accents should be celebrated or wiped out.

Prepare a short presentation on your views about regional accents to open the debate. You need to think about:

- whether you are in favour of or opposed to regional accents
- **why** you are in favour of or opposed to them. For example, because they sound nice? Because they are part of your identity? What would be the benefits of everyone taking elocution lessons (lessons in which you are taught a particular style of speaking)? Give good reasons for your argument.
- what your opponents' arguments will be and how you will counter them
- whether judgements about people based on their accent are fair or accurate.

5 features of spoken language

Learning objective

I am learning:
• about some of the technical features of spoken language.

At GCSE ...

At GCSE you will need to identify and comment on features of spoken language.

You will know some linguistic features, such as what nouns, adjectives, verbs and adverbs are. Spoken language has some features all of its own that you may not have met yet. Here are some important terms that will be useful when you start GCSE.

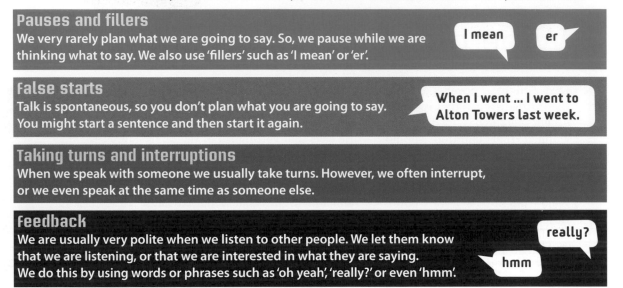

Pauses and fillers

We very rarely plan what we are going to say. So, we pause while we are thinking what to say. We also use 'fillers' such as 'I mean' or 'er'.

I mean   er

False starts

Talk is spontaneous, so you don't plan what you are going to say. You might start a sentence and then start it again.

When I went ... I went to Alton Towers last week.

Taking turns and interruptions

When we speak with someone we usually take turns. However, we often interrupt, or we even speak at the same time as someone else.

Feedback

We are usually very polite when we listen to other people. We let them know that we are listening, or that we are interested in what they are saying. We do this by using words or phrases such as 'oh yeah', 'really?' or even 'hmm'.

really?

hmm

Activity 1 Get ready for GCSE

Look at the following examples of spoken language. Copy the table and label the linguistic feature that has been highlighted each time.

Spoken language examples	Linguistic feature
John: Are you coming down town? Nicky: I want to, I mean, it would be fun.	
Lloyd: Then I ran 30 metres with the ball. Percy: Oh yeah. Lloyd: And passed to Phil.	
Kate: So, he said to me, 'Where did you ...' Lynn: Do you fancy him? Kate: Listen. He said to me, 'Where did you get that hat?' I didn't know what to say.	
David: Tomorrow, well, later this week I'm definitely going to do my homework.	

Activity 2 Get going with GCSE

1. If you are able to, make a recording of 1 minute of a discussion between yourself and a friend. Discuss **one** of the following subjects:
   - I look good in school uniform.
   - School meals are better than the food we get at home.

   a. Play back the conversation. How many of the features of spoken language from page 72 you can identify.

   b. If you can't record a conversation, work in groups of three. Two people should talk about one of the subjects above while the third person should write down any of the features of spoken language they can identify.

Activity 3 Get ahead at GCSE

At GCSE you will need to identify features of spoken language and then think about what those features might reveal about the speaker(s). Look again at your conversation from Activity 2.

1. Which features of spontaneous speech appear frequently in your conversation?

2. What kind of speaker do you think you are? Look at the features you have used in the conversation to write a profile about yourself as a speaker. You could think about:
   - how polite you are as a speaker
   - how good you are at listening and responding
   - how confident you are in this kind of situation
   - whether you blurt things out without thinking or you use techniques to buy time!

ResultsPlus
Top tip

If you record the discussion you can play it back several times to check what the speakers say. This will help you to identify the linguistic features.

Assess yourself

Look back at your answer to Activity 3, question 2. Use the table below to assess your work.

👍 I showed some awareness of what the features showed about me as a speaker.	👍👍 I explained what the features showed about me as a speaker.	👍👍👍 I explained and analysed what the features showed about me as a speaker.

Now look at the grade descriptions below. They show what you will need to do at GCSE.

Grade F	Grade C	Grade A
Students show some awareness of how they use spoken language.	Students explain and evaluate how they use spoken language.	Students explain in detail and give a persuasive evaluation of how they use spoken language.

6 Cracking the code

learning objective

I am learning:
• to understand and write about transcripts.

At GCSE ...

At GCSE you will need to understand what a transcript shows you about spoken language.

Transcripts

There is a way to show the features of spoken language. It is called a transcript. To understand a transcript you need to know some of the symbols used and what they mean. Otherwise it would be like reading a map without a key. These are some of the rules of writing a transcript:

● Do not include any punctuation such as commas, full stops or question marks.
● Show a short pause with (.).
● Show a longer pause with (3) for example, writing the length of the pause in seconds inside the brackets.
● Show when two people are talking at the same time by placing a vertical line at the beginning and at the end of what they say at the same time.
● Underline any words that a speaker emphasises.

Activity 1 Get ready for GCSE

1 Look at the transcript below. It is a transcript of a conversation between two teenage boys.

2 Label any transcript features you can see. For example, can you see any:
● pauses
● overlaps
● emphasis of particular words?

3 Compare your notes with someone else in the classroom. Did you make a list of the same features?

4 Practise reading the transcript out loud, paying attention to the symbols in the transcript.

Chris:	Hey man
Mike:	Sup buddy
Chris:	How'd the date go last night
Mike:	Alright Went to the cinema (.) watched |Toy Soldier 3|
Chris:	|Great film|
Mike:	Yeah (2) It was a good night
Chris:	And
Mike:	We went I mean we were Yeah (2) It was good

Writing about transcripts

At GCSE, once you've identified features of spoken language, you will need to think about what these features might tell you about the speakers. Look at the advice in the table below.

What I need to do	Why I need to do it
Identify features you can see in the transcript.	You need to show you can decode a transcript.
Explain what these features tell you about the conversation.	Explanation is a higher level skill at GCSE.
Comment on the relationship between the two speakers.	Relationships between speakers will affect the way they speak to each other.

Activity 2 Get ahead at GCSE

Below is the rest of the conversation that you studied in Activity 1. Read it through carefully and then write a paragraph about the transcript using the advice in the table above. You might start your answer like this:

> This conversation is between two friends so we should expect the language to be informal. They greet each other. 'Hey man' and 'Sup buddy' which is very informal.

Results Plus
Top tip

Don't just identify linguistic features, such as 'The two boys talk at the same time.' Say something about them, like: 'This shows that Chris has got excited about what Mike is saying.'

Chris: You going to see her again

Mike: Yeah We're going to the school |disco|

Chris: |Disco| Excellent I'm going as well

Mike: You're not are you (.) I hope you're not going to take the mick

Chris: What do you mean

Mike: You know <u>exactly</u> what I mean (.) When you saw me with Sue (.) when I went out with her (.) you kept asking really embarrassing questions in front of her It made me sound like a right idiot

Chris: What like

Mike: One question (.) one question was (.) it was (.) |have you two kissed yet|

Chris: |Oh yeah| (.) That was a laugh

7 Collecting data

learning objective

I am learning:
• how to collect my own spoken language data.

You might think that collecting data is something that only happens in Maths and Science. Well, part of exploring spoken language is collecting examples yourself. This is a unique chance to study language of your choice, such as your own language, or that of your friends, family or on the television.

Activity 1 Get ready for GCSE

A group discussion can be a great way of collecting spoken language data. You will have been asked to discuss issues and topics in lessons.

Read the example below. Students were asked to plan a class discussion on the following topic:

Why do girls outperform boys at GCSE?

To help them carry out an effective discussion, students drew up the following plan:

How many people in each group?

Should groups be a mix of boys and girls?

Should someone make notes as well, just in case?

How will we organise the groups?

Do we have recording facilities?

How many groups?

Group discussion

How will we record the discussion?

Will people run out of ideas?

What problems might we face?

Will the recording be good enough?

Do we need rules? Should someone be in charge?

Will everyone talk at once?

1 Plan your own group discussion.

  a Think of your own question to form the basis of a group discussion – this could be on anything you think other students will have an opinion on.

  b Use the spider diagram above to help plan your discussion.

2 If you have time, carry out your discussion.

  a How successful was it?

  b What would you do differently next time?

Activity 2 Get going with GCSE

Another way to get some spoken language data would be to use conversations that have already been recorded – on the television, YouTube, BBC iplayer and so on. For example, you could look at:

- an interview on a TV or radio chat show
- a more formal interview, such as a news or political interview
- a cookery programme such as *Ready Steady Cook*.

1 **Make a list of different places that you could get spoken language that has already been recorded.**

2 a **Choose one of these examples of recorded spoken language that you would like to analyse.**

b **Write down any problems you might have in analysing the example you have chosen. Think about:**

- how long the recording will be available
- how clear the sound is
- how many people are involved
- how easy it will be to write a transcript of around 30 seconds.

Activity 3 Get ahead at GCSE

At GCSE you can gather and record your own data. Making a transcript is one possible way of doing this.

1 **Make a transcript of about 30 seconds of an example of spoken language. Making a transcript will help you analyse the example.**

2 **Make a list of any problems that you had while making the transcript and how you solved them.**

3 **Were there any problems that you could not solve?**

4 **You've been asked to write an advice sheet for the publication *An Idiot's Guide to Spoken Language*. Write your advice sheet on how best to collect and transcribe data. You could organise this under the 'Do' and 'Don't' headings below.**

Do	Don't
Make sure the recording is good enough quality.	Use an example that involves lots of different speakers.

Results Plus
Top tip

Thirty seconds of transcription should give you some meaningful data to analyse. If you try to do much more than this it will take a long time to transcribe and even longer to analyse. Start small!

8 Analysing informal language

Learning objective

I am learning:
- how to analyse an extract of informal spoken language.

At GCSE ...

At GCSE you can analyse spoken language as part of your controlled assessment.

In the previous lesson you considered how you could get hold of examples of spoken language to analyse. In this lesson you get the chance to really explore what some examples of informal spoken language show you.

Activity 1 Get ready for GCSE

Four students were asked to discuss why girls get better GCSE marks than boys. The student below has started to annotate the discussion. Look at what they have written about the informal spoken language and then complete the annotation by filling in the empty boxes. Use the hints to help you.

> This is quite formal and suggests that Julie thinks that she's important. The 2 second pause suggests that now that she has got everyone's attention she has to think of something to say.

Hint: What do the vertical lines tell you?

Hint: Why does Ravi use LOL? What does it tell you about his tone?

Hint: What do the two hesitations suggest?

Hint: What has happened here

Hint: What do the vertical lines tell you here?

Julie: It's quite obvious (2) Yes it's obvious that in class (2) girls work harder than boys

Alyssa: That's because we're more |mature|

Ravi: |That's| not true

Harry: |I disagree|

Ravi: I think that girls just <u>look</u> as though they're working harder. The boys work hard but want to have a laugh (.) Look how many girls get mobiles taken because they're texting during lessons! They're not working very hard are they LOL

Julie: That's possibly true (2) But why do you think we get better GCSE grades than you

Ravi: Because (2) because (2) you write neater That's it The examiner likes neat writing so he gives girls' writing better marks

Alyssa: |You|

Julie: |Don't get| wound up He's talking rubbish Right Ravi (.) so why do girls get better grades for coursework <u>even when</u> it's done on the compute

Ravi: (4) |Well|

Harry: |Yeah| I think that you're right girls <u>do</u> work harder than boys

Hint: What does the underlining tell you about the way Julie answered Ravi?

Hint: Is this formal language?

Activity 2 Get going with GCSE

At GCSE you will need to explore what spoken language reveals about the speakers.

In this activity you are going to write about the relationships between the people in Activity 1.

1 a Look at the flow chart below.

b Use the hints on the right-hand side to help you complete the table at the bottom of the page.

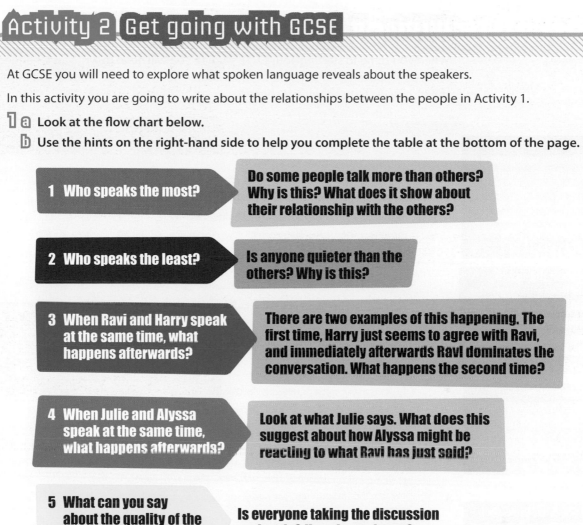

1 Who speaks the most?

Do some people talk more than others? Why is this? What does it show about their relationship with the others?

2 Who speaks the least?

Is anyone quieter than the others? Why is this?

3 When Ravi and Harry speak at the same time, what happens afterwards?

There are two examples of this happening. The first time, Harry just seems to agree with Ravi, and immediately afterwards Ravi dominates the conversation. What happens the second time?

4 When Julie and Alyssa speak at the same time, what happens afterwards?

Look at what Julie says. What does this suggest about how Alyssa might be reacting to what Ravi has just said?

5 What can you say about the quality of the discussion so far?

Is everyone taking the discussion seriously? How do you know?

Question	Answer
Who speaks the most?	
Who speaks the least?	
When Ravi and Harry speak at the same time, what happens afterwards?	
When Julie and Alyssa speak at the same time, what happens afterwards?	
What can you say about the quality of the discussion so far?	

Writing it up

When you come to starting your GCSE studies, you will need to write an extended analysis of spoken language. Here is an example of how a GCSE student did this for the discussion transcribed in Activity 1.

The opening paragraph explains the background to the conversation and then says what linguistic features we might expect from this particular conversation. This is a good way to start the analysis.

The rest of the answer works its way through what is said, almost in sequence. This is one way to structure a good response. Another might be to look at each speaker in turn.

There is a lot of good analysis in this paragraph. The student isn't just identifying features – they are commenting on what those features tell them.

The student shows they understand and can apply terms such as 'false starts' and 'hesitations'.

The student continues to analyse the conversation thoroughly.

In this conversation there are four speakers in a reasonably formal situation, in a classroom. We might expect some formal language, but because the conversation is spontaneous there is also likely to be informal language. Because there are four speakers we might also expect to see interruptions and examples of speakers talking at the same time.

Julie starts the conversation off with 'It's quite obvious' which is quite formal and suggests that Julie thinks that she is important. She takes a lead role in the discussion, always trying to get the boys to take part seriously. The two second pause suggests that now she has everyone's attention she has to think of something to say.

Alyssa makes the comment that girls are more mature, but the boys feel so strongly about this that they both speak over her. Ravi then takes on the conversation. He doesn't seem to be taking the conversation very seriously because he finishes off with 'LOL'. He has used text speak in a conversation to say that it is funny that girls get their mobile phones confiscated in lessons. This informal language suggests that Ravi is not taking the discussion seriously.

Julie realises that Ravi is not taking the discussion very seriously so she says, 'But why do you think...' to encourage Ravi to say something serious. Ravi starts his response off with a false start and two hesitations, which suggests that he is desperately trying to think of something to say. The use of the phrase 'That's it' shows that he is pleased with what he has managed to think of.

Alyssa gets cross because Ravi is still not taking the discussion seriously, and interrupts him with 'You' but Julie realises that Ravi is only trying to get the girls angry and interrupts Alyssa to stop her from getting angry, although the informal phrase 'He's talking rubbish' suggests that Julie is also getting angry. Julie's comment, 'Right Ravi' is another attempt to get Ravi to say something sensible. Ravi tries to say something but Harry interrupts and speaks over him. Harry seems to be embarrassed about Ravi's contribution to the discussion and wants to agree with the girls.

Activity 3 | Get ahead at GCSE

Glossary

context: background information, the circumstances that form the setting for something

Now choose your own example of informal spoken language. This could be something you collected in the previous lesson or a new example.

1 Transcribe around 30 seconds then annotate the transcript.

2 Now write about 200–300 words analysing your example of spoken language. Here are some hints to help you with your analysis:

- Start off with an introductory paragraph giving the **context** or background information of the conversation and what linguistic features you might expect to see.
- Decide whether you want to go through the conversation in sequence, or whether you want to focus on one person at a time.
- Once you've identified any features, always ask yourself 'what does this suggest about the speaker?'

Results Plus
Top tip

Don't just identify features. Always think about and try to explain what those features tell you.

Assess yourself

Look back at your answer to Activity 3. Use the table below to assess your work.

👍 I made general comments about spoken language, but only included a few examples.	👍👍 I used some examples to support my general comments about spoken language.	👍👍👍 I used frequent, relevant examples to support my points.

Now look at the grade descriptions below. They show what you will need to do at GCSE.

Grade **F**	Grade **C**	Grade **A**
Students refer to specific details when justifying their views.	Students refer to specific details to support their analysis of spoken language.	Students use a range of details to give a persuasive evaluation of spoken language.

ResultsPlus
Be the examiner!

In this activity you are going to look at some extracts from sample answers to Activity 3 on page 81. An examiner has commented on the extracts and suggested a grade, but he has not shown which comment belongs to which extract.

Your task:
- Read the different student answer extracts.
- As you read, think about the strengths and weaknesses of the answers.
- Read the examiner's comments.
- Work out which comment belongs to which answer.

Like a real examiner, you could be asked to explain your choices so make sure you have reasons ready to support your answers.

Extract from student answer 1   Grade

This is a conversation between four people set up during a lesson. Because there are so many people there are going to be interruptions. Because it is a discussion there will be hesitations and false starts. We can see an example of a false start and a hesitation in the very first sentence. Julie starts to answer the question with 'It's quite obvious' then there is a two second hesitation and she starts again with 'Yes, it's obvious...' An example of an interruption is when at the end of the transcript when Ravi has a long hesitation and says 'Well' but Harry helps him out by interrupting him and agreeing with Julie's point. Ravi pauses for so long because he doesn't really know the answer. I think Harry seems to sense this and he comes to his friend's rescue. Or maybe he felt awkward at the long silence so felt the need to say something.

Extract from student answer 2   Grade

This is a discussion about why girls get better GCSE results than boys. I don't really agree with the statement as some boys are very intelligent but this is what the conversation is about. The boys don't do themselves any favours in this conversation because they mostly come across as a bit daft and not really taking it very serious but the girls take it more seriously and seem to win the argument. Julie tries to sound a bit posh at the start like when she says 'It's quite obvious' which seems a bit formal and like she's trying to make a point. Alyssa doesn't say much maybe she's just quiet. Harry doesn't add much.

Extract from student answer 3   Grade (?)

In this discussion we can see lots of features of spoken language. For example, Julie hesitates when she speaks at the beginning. It's also a bit of a false start too. Ravi and Harry speak at the same time too. Later, when Ravi has been asked a question he also pauses for a long time and then doesn't even answer! Harry answers instead but not very well. There are also some interruptions, like when Alyssa is about to complain and Julie interrupts her.

E Examiner comment 1

This extract from the student's answer is typical of E grade performance. There is some irrelevant material here which has nothing to do with spoken language analysis and is a waste of time. A more effective opening would have been to contextualise the conversation. One feature of spoken language is picked out – the formal nature of Julie's opening words – but the student doesn't really go on to explain why Julie chooses this formality, and much of the answer talks in general terms without picking out specific features. If the student sustained this level in the rest of their response, they would most likely achieve a grade E.

D Examiner comment 2

This extract from the student's answer is typical of D grade performance. The candidate has not given much thought to the context of the dialogue. While there are some comments about the features found in spoken language, the examples are often generalised. More specific examples would have improved this extract, as would some commentary on what those features show us. There is no analysis or explanation of the features of spoken language in this extract. If the student sustained this level throughout their response, it is likely that they would achieve a grade D.

C Examiner comment 3

This extract from the student's answer is typical of C grade performance. The candidate has a better understanding of the context. They identify features found in spoken language and give relevant examples from the transcript. There is some analysis and explanation, such as when the candidate explains why Harry interrupts Ravi. If the student sustained this type of writing throughout their response, they would probably achieve a grade C. However, more analysis and less description would have improved this answer.

---

1 Now look at your own answer to Activity 3. Compare It to the three extracts from student answers on page 82.
   • Which one is your answer closest to?
   • Discuss or jot down what you might need to do to improve your answer if you were to do it again.

9 Analysing formal spoken language

Learning objective

I am learning:
• how to analyse an extract of formal spoken language.

At GCSE …

At GCSE you can analyse different styles of spoken language for your controlled assessment.

In the previous lesson you analysed an example of informal spoken language. At GCSE you could also analyse a piece of formal spoken language.

Activity 1 Get ready for GCSE

Read the transcript below. A Year Head is talking to a girl about her behaviour during a lesson earlier in the day.

A student has already started to annotate the example of formal spoken language but has not finished the job. Look at what they have written and then complete the annotation by filling in all of the empty comment boxes.

This is a very formal start to the conversation. The Year Head is emphasising her superiority.

Year Head:	So Caroline You had a bit of a problem lesson three with Mrs Alderhaye
Caroline:	Yes miss
Year Head:	And how do you feel about your behaviour now
Caroline:	I'm very sorry miss (.) It won't happen again
Year Head:	So what actually did happen
Caroline:	Nothing miss
Year Head:	But Mrs Alderhaye says that you swore |at her|
Caroline:	|No miss That's not true|
Year Head:	So what is your side of the story
Caroline:	Miss she does my |head in|
Year Head:	|Caroline|
Caroline:	Well she does (2) miss
Year Head:	So (.) tell me exactly what happened
Caroline:	I was doing all my work miss and I (.) well I (.) I was listening to my music but she caught me She shouted at me and told me to 'Hand it over' I felt like a <u>criminal</u> (.) In front of <u>everyone</u> (2) I said she was <u>pathetic</u> and she kicked me out
Year Head:	I see

This example of informal language suggests that Caroline has got angry. She started off calmly, talking formally, like her Year Head, but here she seems to lose her control.

Activity 2 Get going with GCSE

You are now going to write about the relationship between the two people in the example of spoken language that you have just annotated. Copy the table below and then answer the questions.

Question	Answer
In this extract the speakers take turns to speak. What does this suggest about the conversation?	
There are some examples of the two speakers talking at the same time. When does this happen?	
What examples are there of formal and informal language? What does this suggest about the relationship between the speakers?	

Activity 3 Get ahead at GCSE

1 **Look again at the transcript from Activity 1. Imagine that the conversation happened in a slightly different way. For example:**
- Caroline becomes the dominant speaker.
- The Year Head apologises for Mrs Alderhaye's behaviour.

Take one of these new possibilities and re-write the transcript of the conversation.

2 **Make notes on your new transcript showing what you have changed and why you have changed it.**

Assess yourself

Look back at your answer to Activity 2. Use the table below to assess your work.

👍 I made general comments about spoken language, but only included a few examples.	👍👍 I used some examples to support my general comments about spoken language.	👍👍👍 I used frequent, relevant examples to support my points.

Now look at the grade descriptions below. They show what you will need to do at GCSE.

Grade **F**	Grade **C**	Grade **A**
Students refer to specific details when justifying their views.	Students refer to specific details to support their analysis of spoken language.	Students use a range of details to give a persuasive evaluation of spoken language.

10 Soaps

learning objective

I am learning:
• how talk is 'represented' in the media.

At GCSE ...

At GCSE you will write for the spoken voice – a soap opera is an example of a text written for the spoken voice.

Writers of TV dramas such as soap operas spend a lot of time creating characters that the audience will feel are realistic. A major part of creating realistic characters is making their talk sound realistic. This kind of spoken language is called 'scripted' or 'represented' speech.

Activity 1 Get ready for GCSE

There are a huge variety of soap operas on TV, attracting millions of viewers every week. Most soaps share some common ingredients, but do you know what they are?

Think about some popular soaps. What features do they have in common? Think about:

- The setting – where do soaps usually take place?
- Characters – what kind of people are usually involved?
- Plots and events – what kinds of things usually happen in soaps?
- Mood – do happy or tragic things happen to the characters?
- Structure – how are soaps usually structured?

Activity 2 Get going with GCSE

A TV script includes some features that you may not have come across before. Look at the example script on page 87.

1 The first scene has been annotated for you. Look at the second scene and annotate any features of script writing you can see.

2 A good scriptwriter makes made-up characters sound believable. They do this by using the features of spontaneous language in their writing.

a How far do you think the script sounds like spontaneous speech? Annotate the script, picking out any features of spontaneous language. For example can you find any examples of hesitations, false starts, pauses, overlaps, fillers, repetition and so on?

b Write another ten lines of dialogue for this episode. It could describe Mona and Thomas' reaction to the news of Clio's death. Make sure you:
  - use the features of a TV script
  - make your characters sound realistic by using features of spontaneous language.

Activity 2 continued...

Glossary

INT.: interior, inside of
SFX: sound effects

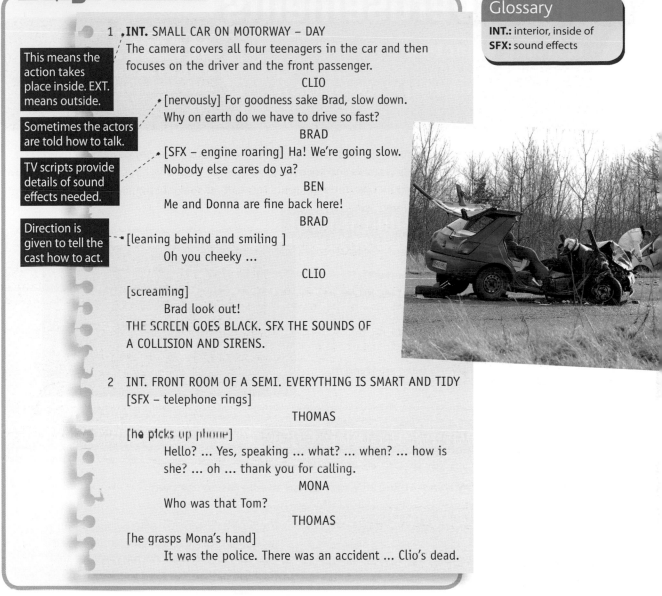

1 **INT.** SMALL CAR ON MOTORWAY – DAY
The camera covers all four teenagers in the car and then focuses on the driver and the front passenger.

CLIO
[nervously] For goodness sake Brad, slow down. Why on earth do we have to drive so fast?

BRAD
[SFX – engine roaring] Ha! We're going slow. Nobody else cares do ya?

BEN
Me and Donna are fine back here!

BRAD
[leaning behind and smiling]
Oh you cheeky ...

CLIO
[screaming]
Brad look out!
THE SCREEN GOES BLACK. SFX THE SOUNDS OF A COLLISION AND SIRENS.

2 INT. FRONT ROOM OF A SEMI. EVERYTHING IS SMART AND TIDY
[SFX – telephone rings]

THOMAS
[he picks up phone]
Hello? ... Yes, speaking ... what? ... when? ... how is she? ... oh ... thank you for calling.

MONA
Who was that Tom?

THOMAS
[he grasps Mona's hand]
It was the police. There was an accident ... Clio's dead.

This means the action takes place inside. EXT. means outside.

Sometimes the actors are told how to talk.

TV scripts provide details of sound effects needed.

Direction is given to tell the cast how to act.

Activity 3 Get ahead at GCSE

At GCSE, you need to be able to write effectively for the spoken voice. Effective writing focuses on the purpose and audience of the writing.

1 **Write an episode of your favourite soap following the producer's brief opposite:**

I want someone to come in and shock everyone with a piece of news. There must be an argument about a relative. For the cliff hanger someone should collapse and look as though they are dead. Include at least four people.

First decide on:
● who will be involved
● what the piece of news will be and what the argument will be about
● how you will make the speech of your characters sound realistic.

2 **When you have finished, annotate your script to explain to the producer why the choices you have made will result in characters the audience can believe in.**

11 TV advertisements

Learning objective

I am learning:
• how to structure and write a TV advertisement.

At GCSE ...

At GCSE you will need to show you know how to structure a text correctly.

You will probably watch a number of television adverts every day. Most adverts last about thirty seconds and encourage you to do something – such as watch a TV show or buy a product. So, the purpose of most TV adverts is to persuade the audience.

Activity 1 Get ready for GCSE

1 **What makes a good television advert?**

a **Make a list of your favourite TV adverts.**

b **What is it that makes them your favourite? Are they funny, unusual, shocking, or something else?**

c **Do your chosen adverts have anything in common?**

Activity 2 Get going with GCSE

Look at the advice below about writing a TV advert from an advertising company.

1 A television advertisement should have a beginning, a middle and an end. It is like a very short film. The advertisement should tell a story about the product that is being sold.

2 All of the decisions that you make about the advertisement should be aimed at your target audience. For example, if you are selling baby nappies who is your target audience?

3 In your script use the following pattern:

• **Say what you want to say**
Your first sentence, or lead sentence, is like a headline. It should be punchy and grab your audience's attention.

Say exactly what product you are advertising. For example you might say 'Buy Triple X Fruit Juice'. You will need to think about the tone of your advertisement. For example, will it be noisy, sexy or serious?

• **Explain what you mean**
At this stage of the advertisement you should give examples to support what you have said in your lead sentence. So, if you have said that people should buy Triple X Fruit Juice, you could then explain that it has 30% more fruit than other brands; that the fruit is all collected carefully by hand in the Caribbean; that all fruit used is Fair Trade fruit.

• **Say it all again**
Your audience is unlikely to be deliberately watching your advertisement. So, they might have missed the beginning. Say the lead line again, possibly in a slightly different way. At this stage you might even tell your audience where they can buy the product.

• **Be persuasive**
Remember that the purpose of your advertisement is to persuade people. So you need to use features of persuasive language such as rhetorical questions, patterns of three, repetition and emotive language.

Activity 2 continued...

1 Plan out an advertisement to sell Triple X Fruit Juice. Create a storyboard using up to ten 'frames' like the one below.

a In the box on the left, describe exactly what the audience will see in the scene.

b In the box on the right, write the words that the audience will hear and details of any sounds or music that they will hear.

Frame number _____

Words _____

_____

_____

Sounds / music _____

_____

_____

Activity 3 Get ahead at GCSE

Your task is to produce a TV advert. To do this you need to go through the following process.

1 Make up a product. In five sentences describe your product and why people should buy it.

2 Carry out some research: take the description of your product to other people in the class and ask them why they would or wouldn't buy the product.

3 Use the reasons why people **would** buy your product in your advertisement. Don't mention the reasons why people **wouldn't** buy your product.

4 Use the structure that you learnt about in Activity 2 to plan out your advert.

5 Shoot it!

Assess yourself

Look at the advert you created in Activity 3. Use the table below to assess your work.

👍 I wrote the script for a TV advert, describing my product and using some persuasive features.	👍👍 I wrote a carefully structured script using a number of persuasive features.	👍👍👍 I carefully chose language, rhetorical techniques and music and sounds in my advert to persuade my audience.

Now look at the grade descriptions below. They show you what you will need to do at GCSE.

Grade F	Grade C	Grade A
Students' ideas are clearly and simply communicated to the reader with some variety of vocabulary.	Students use a range of techniques and vocabulary to create effects and engage the reader.	Students skilfully structure their texts, using a range of techniques and imaginative vocabulary to hold the reader's interest.

12 Documentaries

learning objective

I am learning:
• to use vocabulary and sentence structure effectively in my writing for the spoken voice.

At GCSE ...

At GCSE you will need to vary your vocabulary and sentence structure when writing creatively.

Documentary programmes focus on one issue and provide an argument about that issue. For example, a documentary might argue that people still use their mobile phones while driving and so the £60 fine for offenders should be increased to £150.

Activity 1 Get ready for GCSE

Read the following extract from a documentary written by Sophie Taylor. While you are reading it look at the comments about the language that Sophie has used.

Script	Visuals
Music hold for twenty seconds: *This Used to be my Playground* by Madonna.	
Producer: My name is Sophie Taylor and today I am investigating the way the local town council has wasted an enormous amount of money on a play park that nobody wanted, and nobody uses. Against the advice of all the local people, the council still went ahead with the park. I have uncovered some startling facts. Facts that will make your blood boil.	Close up on Sophie Taylor.
	Pan over to play park on Sophie Taylor's right.
Let's go back to the start of this project, and the public hearing that was held on 12 March 2009. Sharon Baldwyn, you were a Councillor at the time, and you were present at the planning meeting. What do you recall of the meeting?	Sophie Taylor outside town hall, then move back to take in Sophie Taylor and Sharon Baldwyn.
Sharon Baldwyn: It was over a year ago but I still remember it clearly. There were ten people from families whose houses overlook the site of the play park. Even though they all had children they were opposed to the park.	Close up on Sharon Baldwyn.
Producer: Why was that?	
Sharon Baldwyn: Because they would have had to cross a busy main road, with their young children, to get to the park. Not practical. Not practical at all.	

Introduces herself to the audience.

Use of the word 'enormous' to exaggerate how much money has been 'wasted'.

Explains clearly what the subject of the documentary is.

Formal language to make the documentary more convincing.

A short sentence and use of emotive language help emphasise Sophie's argument.

Interview with expert to make the argument more convincing.

Two short sentences and repetition of 'not practical' help emphasise the idea that the park was a waste of time and money.

Activity 1 continued...

Write another ten lines for this documentary following the guidelines below.

- Include an interview with another person.
- Try to use some short sentences for effect.
- Choose your vocabulary so that it has a real impact on the reader.
- The producer should use formal language when she speaks.
- The person who she interviews may talk less formally.
- Remember to include the visuals for the film crew.

Activity 2 Get going with GCSE

You are now going to write the opening of your own television documentary.

1 First choose one of the three briefs below.

> Brief 1: Choose a topic that is important at school. For example, you could argue that you should not have school uniform, or that homework should be banned.

> Brief 2: Choose a topic that is important for your local area. For example, you could argue that the facilities for teenagers need to be improved.

> Brief 3: Choose any topic that is important to you, regardless of whether it is about your local area or school or something else. For example, are you fed up with how teenagers are portrayed in the media?

2 Once you have chosen your subject, plan your documentary thoroughly. Think about:

- How you will introduce the documentary.
- What language features you will use (such as emotive language, repetition, and so on) to emphasise your points.
- How you might vary the length of your sentences for effect.
- How many people will be involved in the documentary.
- What visuals you would want to include as part of the documentary.

3 Once you have planned your documentary thoroughly, write it up.

Activity 3 Get ahead at GCSE

At GCSE the examiner will need to be able to find examples of you having used well-chosen vocabulary and varied sentences to make your writing more effective.

Look at your completed documentary script from Activity 2. Annotate your script to show where you have:
- used emotive language
- varied your sentence length
- suggested visuals that will help give the documentary impact.

In this activity you are going to look at some extracts from sample answers to Activity 2 on page 91. An examiner has commented on the extracts and suggested a grade, but he has not shown which comment belongs to which extract.

Your task:
- Read the different student answer extracts.
- As you read, think about the strengths and weaknesses of the answers.
- Read the examiner's comments.
- Work out which comment belongs to which answer.

Like a real examiner, you could be asked to explain your choices so make sure you have reasons ready to support your answers.

Extract from student answer 1   Grade (?)

Script	Visuals
Presenter: Look at that. Would you want your children playing on that? I think that that is dangerous. Don't you? Would you want your children playing in this play park? I know I wouldn't. I have been looking into play parks in Somerville. They are not very good. I have seen broken swings, like that one, and broken slides. I have even seen broken glass. I interviewed someone from the Council about this. I asked him what he was going to do about it.	Broken swing Change to presenter
Graham Vaughan: Hello.	Camera on Graham Vaughan
Presenter: What are you going to do about it?	Camera on Presenter
Graham Vaughan: Because of money we have difficulty doing much. We have already started cleaning up the litter and we will fix the swings as soon as we can.	Camera on Graham Vaughan

Extract from student answer 2   Grade (?)

Script	Visuals
Music for thirty seconds: *Money* by The Beatles.	Images of teenagers in a shopping mall Fade to presenter
Presenter: Hello. My name is John Smith and this week's investigation is into teenagers' pocket money. Did you realise that recent research by the BBC has discovered that on average teenagers are given over £1,000 per year in pocket money! This means that teenagers make a massive annual five billion pound contribution to the economy. I spoke to some teenagers about how they spend their pocket money. Here is what Chris said.	
Chris: I get paid £10 per week pocket money, but I have to earn it. It's not a gift. I have to babysit my younger sister once a week when my parents go out, and I wash both my parents' cars.	Medium shot of Chris in his bedroom, with lots of electronic gadgets around the room

Script	Visuals
Presenter: Hello. I have been asking teenagers in Warford about the facilities that are provided for them. I have been shocked by what they have had to say.	Close up on presenter
Mary: We used to have a Youth Club but when things got broken they weren't repaired. We did try to do it ourselves but we couldn't raise enough money. We did get a small grant from the council but it wasn't enough; they had other priorities I think. But the Youth Club did keep loads of teens off the streets. Now we just wander around the streets at night.	Close up on Mary

E Examiner comment 1

This extract from the student's answer is typical of E grade performance. There is some evidence that the student understands the purpose and audience, but the introduction is brief and inappropriate. Also, the visual prompts are limited. The style is appropriate for a documentary but the vocabulary is limited. The spelling is accurate. Simple sentence structures are used. If the student sustained this type of writing throughout their response, they would probably achieve a grade E.

D Examiner comment 2

This extract from the student's answer is typical of D grade performance. There is a clear sense of purpose. For example, the purpose of the programme is mentioned at the beginning. The visual prompts are limited, but there is some awareness of close-up shots. The style is appropriate for a documentary and there are signs of a range of vocabulary. Spelling is accurate. Sentence structures are beginning to be used to convey meaning. If the student sustained this level in the rest of their response, they would most likely achieve a grade D.

C Examiner comment 3

This extract from the student's answer is typical of C grade performance. There is a clear sense of purpose and audience. For example, the presenter introduces themselves as well as the subject of the documentary. The subject seems to have been researched which increases its credibility. The visual prompts help to give the impression that this script has been carefully considered. There is a range of vocabulary and a range of punctuation which controls sentence structures. If the student sustained this level throughout their response, it is likely that they would achieve a grade C.

---

1 Now look at your own documentary. Compare it to the extracts from three student answers on these pages.
  a Which one is your answer closest to?
  b Discuss or jot down what you might need to do to improve your answer if you were to do it again.

Unit 4
Get Creative

The chances are that, in the last week, you will have read or listened to lots of different types of creative writing without even realising it. Creative writing can take many different forms, including those below and more:

poetry   limericks   song lyrics   short stories

character voice overs in computer games   novels   play scripts

magazine and newspaper articles   television adverts

Producing good creative writing is a gradual process. A skilful writer gathers ideas, plans the text and then writes and redrafts to make the piece interesting and engaging to the reader, which is no mean feat!

In this unit you will have the chance to read and explore a range of poetry to help you understand how to approach a poem and tease out the writer's meaning. You will also have lots of opportunities to attempt your own pieces of creative writing, including writing:

a description of a fairground

a transcript for a news item

a story based on a poem

an online video advert

What am I learning in this unit?

In this unit you will start to develop some of the following skills that you will need at GCSE.

Reading

I will learn how to:
- respond to an unseen poem.
- analyse the words a poet uses and think about why they were chosen.
- examine the devices a poet uses to explore themes and ideas.
- consider the choices poets make about the rhythm and form of their poem.
- identify a poet's viewpoint and concerns.
- compare two poems.

Writing

I will learn how to:
- plan and write a piece of personal writing using the first person.
- vary my sentence length and vocabulary for effect.
- write creatively for a specific purpose and audience.
- consider forms of writing and how to transform a text from one form to another.
- follow a brief and write a persuasive text.
- check my work and address patterns of error.

Why do I need to know this?

All of the lessons in this unit focus on specific skills that you will eventually be assessed on when you start GCSE English. By practising and developing these skills now you can give yourself a head start so that when you do start GCSE you are prepared and ready to succeed!

1 Unwrapping a poem

Learning objective

I am learning:
• to respond to an unseen poem.

At GCSE ...

At GCSE you will need to say what you think a poem is about and back this up with evidence from the poem.

Activity 1 Get ready for GCSE

At GCSE you will need to be able to read and respond to poems. This could include poems that you might not have read before. There are some easy strategies that can help you do this.

1 Look at the word opposite. What does this word make you think of? Create a spider diagram of any relevant words and images.

Illumination

2 Look at the picture below.

a What words come to mind when you look at this picture?

b What emotions does it make you feel?

Activity 2 Get going with GCSE

1 Now look at the poem called 'Illuminations'. Read the first line and the last line.

a How do the first line and the last line connect with each other?

b How do the first and last lines connect with the title?

ILLUMINATIONS

By Tony Harrison

The two machines on Blackpool's Central Pier,
The Long Drop and *The Haunted House* gave me
my thrills the holiday that post-war year
but my father watched me spend impatiently:

5 *Another tanner's worth, but then no more!*
But I sneaked back the moment that you napped.
50 weeks of ovens, and 6 years of war
made you want sleep and ozone, and you snapped:

Bugger the machines! Breathe God's fresh air!

10 I sulked all week, and wouldn't hold your hand.
I'd never heard you mention God, or swear,
and it took me until now to understand.
I see now all the piled old pence turned green,
enough to hang the murderer all year

15 and stare at millions of ghosts in the machine---
The penny dropped in time! Wish you were here!

Activity 2 continued...

2 Look at the poem's presentation on the page. It uses some italic text. For each line of italic text, complete **one** of the sentence starters below.

This sounds like...

This looks like...

These words suggest...

This makes me think...

A sentence commenting on *'The Long Drop'* in line 2 has been completed for you.

> This makes me think of old-fashioned games and slot machines on the pier. It might be referring to a slot machine where a man is hanged, which the poet suggests in line 14 of the poem.

3 Now read the whole poem. It explores a tension between a young boy and his father. The poet remembers problems he had with his father during a family holiday and his sulky reaction.

Write two lists of words or phrases that the poet uses to show the difference between the father and the son.

Son (youth)	Father (age)
thrills	impatiently

4 How would you describe the boy's mood during the holiday as a result of the tension with his father? Explain it in your own words.

5 Can you explain the poet's mood at the end of the poem now that he is older, looking back at these events? Look again at the title and the last line of the poem to help you.

Activity 3 Get ahead at GCSE

1 Now re-read the whole poem. Look carefully at the final stanza and the last two lines.

2 Write a paragraph explaining why you think the poet chose the title 'Illuminations'.

   a Try to include particular words or phrases from the poem to support your opinion.

   b Look at the model paragraph below on another poem from this unit, to help you with how to structure your response.

> The title of the poem is 'Geography lesson'. This is partly because the poem is about actual Geography lessons. On another level it is also about a more important 'lesson' learnt from his Geography teacher – to explore and make the most of life because life can be short. We know this when the poet says 'a lesson he never knew he taught / Is with me to this day'. Here the poet emphasises that now he travels because of the lesson for life that he learnt from this teacher, who died without exploring the places he talked about.

2 Wordsmithery

Learning objective

I am learning:
• to analyse the words a poet uses and think about why they were chosen.

At GCSE ...

At GCSE you will need to select specific words and phrases and comment on why the poet has chosen them.

Activity 1 Get ready for GCSE

When we are young, the adults in our life often decide things for us that make up our identity. For example our name, our religion, the clothes we wear and so on.

1 Look at the words opposite. Which are most important for your feeling of identity?

2 Would you add anything to this list?

Accent and dialect

Fashion and appearance

Items you own

Religion

Family

Friends

Music

Leisure interests

Place of birth

Activity 2 Get going with GCSE

1 The list of words opposite is taken from the poem you are going to study in this activity. Read the words and then answer the following questions:

ⓐ Can you see any links between the words the poet has chosen?

ⓑ Which words are repeated most?

ⓒ What does this tell you about what the poem is about?

An example has been done for you.

2 Think of two questions you would like to ask the poet as a result of looking at her choice of language.

3 Now read the poem on page 99. What are your first impressions about the topic of the poem and what the poet is worried about? Gather some ideas by looking at:
● the title
● the first line and the last lines
● the poet's use of italic text and layout.

accent accent awful back
back back back back blood boil bones buried
call calling cones coul crabbit cream cried
day dead disappeared dour dreadful dreich
eedyit eight English
feel fell forced found
geggie ghastly gie gie go
heidbanger
| | | | | | | | | | | | |
knocked
laldie like like like long lost lost lost
ma ma made malkie marched mother's mouth mouth my
my my my my my my my my my my my my my my my
new night not
old old old old opened out own
pokey
quite
sad said scones scotland scottish scottish sea see see
shut singsongy soil soor sound south started stones
strange stretch stummer swallowed swear
taken teuchter thing tongue tongue tongue try turned
ur
vowels
wabbit wandering wanted wanted wanted was was
when when when where whole with word words words
words words words words words words would wrong
yer you you you you you you

These words suggest that the poet is describing something distressing because all these words can be linked to negative emotions

Activity 2 continued...

4 In this poem, the speaker describes how her vocabulary and pronunciation changed as she moved from Scotland to England: 'my vowels grew longer'; 'words fell off my tongue'. She suggests that this change is linked to her physical self – her body.

a Identify the words in the poem that are to do with the body.

b Why do you think the poet links the idea of accent with her physical body?

Old Tongue

By Jackie Kay

When I was eight, I was forced south.
Not long after, when I opened
my mouth, a strange thing happened.
I lost my Scottish accent.
Words fell off my tongue:
eedyit, dreich, wabbit, crabbit
stummer, teuchter, heidbanger,
so you are, so am ur, see you, see ma ma,
shut yer geggie or I'll gie you the malkie!

My own vowels started to stretch like my bones
and I turned my back on Scotland.
Words disappeared in the dead of night,
new words marched in: ghastly, awful,
quite dreadful, *scones* said like *stones.*
Pukey hats into ice cream cones.
Oh where did all my words go —
my old words, my lost words?
Did you ever feel sad when you lost a word,
did you ever try and call it back
like calling in the sea?
If I could have found my words wandering,
I swear I would have taken them in,
swallowed them whole, knocked them back.

Out in the English soil, my old words
buried themselves. It made my mother's blood boil.
I cried one day with the wrong sound in my mouth.
I wanted them back; I wanted my old accent back,
my old tongue. My dour soor Scottish tongue.
Singsongy. I wanted to *gie it laldie*.

Activity 3 Get ahead at GCSE

Glossary

gie it laldie: to do it with energy

Re-read the whole poem, looking carefully at the words the poet has used.

1 Now choose a word from the bank below or one of your own that you think best summarises the central topic of the poem.

I think the central topic of the poem is: Identity Speech

Growing up   Loss   Moving house   Childhood   Change

2 Write a paragraph explaining your choice. Support your views with reference to the poet's use of language.

ResultsPlus
Watch out!

Don't forget to find evidence from the text to back up your point.

3 A poet's tools

learning objective

I am learning:
- to examine the devices a poet uses to explore themes and ideas.

At GCSE ...

At GCSE you may need to identify and comment on how poets use literary devices for effect.

Activity 1 Get ready for GCSE

1 Poets and artists often communicate their ideas by appealing to the senses; smell, touch, sight, sound and taste. Look at the painting below and read the information in the bottom left-hand corner.

a What details can you see in the painting that others might not have spotted?

b Imagine you are at the scene. Write ten phrases that describe experiencing the event through your senses. For example:

I can hear the low wailing of the family.

Use these sentence starters to help you:

1 *I can hear...* **2** *I can see...* **3** *I can smell...* **4** *I can feel...*

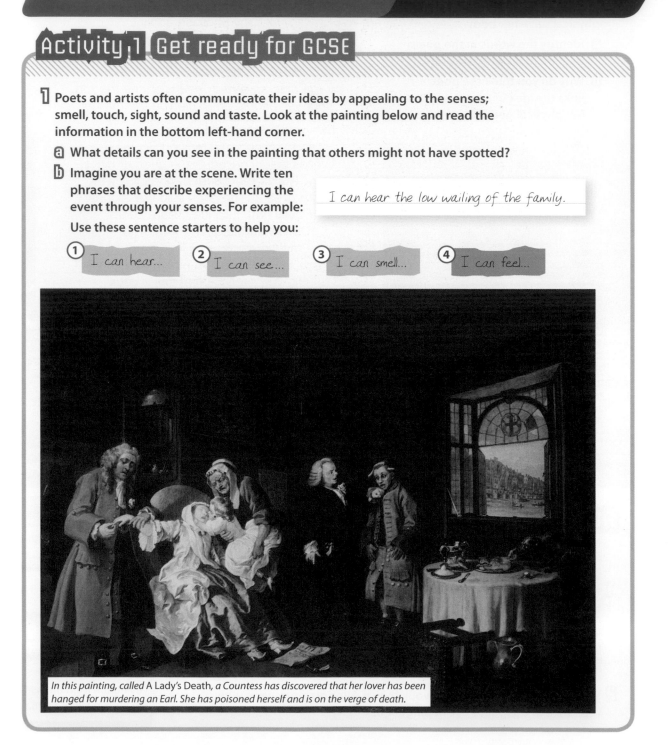

In this painting, called A Lady's Death, a Countess has discovered that her lover has been hanged for murdering an Earl. She has poisoned herself and is on the verge of death.

Activity 1 continued...

2 Now look at the image below. What do you feel when you look at this image? What does it suggest to you? Create a spider diagram of your ideas based on the one below the photograph.

My feelings

A fly

What does the
image suggest?

3 Can you make any connection between the two images? Think about:

a the title of the painting

b what you might associate with a fly.

Activity 2 Get going with GCSE

Read the poem below by Emily Dickinson. In it the poet describes the experience of being about to die.

I HEARD A FLY BUZZ WHEN I DIED

I heard a Fly buzz – when I died –
The Stillness in the Room
Was like the Stillness in the Air –
Between the Heaves of Storm –

5 The Eyes around – had wrung them dry –
And Breaths were gathering firm
For that last Onset – when the King
Be witnessed – in the Room –

I willed my Keepsakes – Signed away
10 What portion of me be
Assignable – and then it was
There interposed a Fly –

With Blue – uncertain – stumbling Buzz –
Between the light – and me –
15 And then the Windows failed – and then
I could not see to see –

Poets often use devices such as similes and metaphors to help get their ideas across. Being able to identify these devices and comment on how they work is a useful skill when you start GCSE. Remember:

- A **simile** is a comparison between two things using 'like' or 'as'. For example, 'His life was like a journey' is a simile.
- A **metaphor** compares two things by suggesting one thing 'is' another. For example 'Life is a journey' is a metaphor.

1 List the things mentioned in the poem that you might expect to see in a 'traditional death scene'.

2 Now consider the language in the famous opening of this poem.

> I heard a Fly buzz – when I died –

  a What is your reaction to the opening line?

  b Does it raise any questions in your mind?

  c Does it reflect the idea of death that you see in the painting on page 100?

3 The poet uses the device of a **simile** to show the atmosphere in the room in the first stanza of the poem. Can you find the simile and explain how two things are being compared?

4 Dickinson uses metaphorical language in the poem.

  a What or who might she be describing as 'the King'? Who might be the king of this scene?

  b What she is referring to in the line 'the Windows failed'?

Activity 3 Get ahead at GCSE

At GCSE you will need to comment on how a poet explores ideas and themes.

1 Re-read the whole poem and think about how Dickinson plays with the idea of death. For example, this is one person's response to the poem.

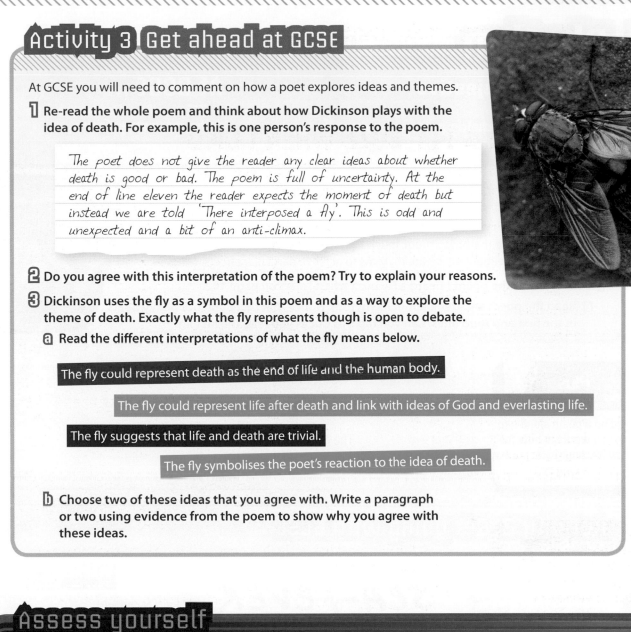

> The poet does not give the reader any clear ideas about whether death is good or bad. The poem is full of uncertainty. At the end of line eleven the reader expects the moment of death but instead we are told 'There interposed a fly'. This is odd and unexpected and a bit of an anti-climax.

2 Do you agree with this interpretation of the poem? Try to explain your reasons.

3 Dickinson uses the fly as a symbol in this poem and as a way to explore the theme of death. Exactly what the fly represents though is open to debate.

a Read the different interpretations of what the fly means below.

The fly could represent death as the end of life and the human body.

The fly could represent life after death and link with ideas of God and everlasting life.

The fly suggests that life and death are trivial.

The fly symbolises the poet's reaction to the idea of death.

b Choose two of these ideas that you agree with. Write a paragraph or two using evidence from the poem to show why you agree with these ideas.

Assess yourself

Look at your answers to Activity 3. Use the table below to assess your work.

| 👍 I made general comments about the ideas and themes in the poem using some evidence. | 👍👍 I made specific points about the poem, using evidence from the poem to support my points. | 👍👍👍 I carefully explored the ideas and themes in the poem, using well-chosen details to support my points. |

Now look at the grade descriptions below. They show what you will need to do at GCSE.

Grade F	Grade C	Grade A
Students describe the main ideas or themes in a text, referring to specific aspects of language to support their points.	Students understand the ideas and themes in texts, referring to specific aspects of language to support their points.	Students give imaginative and persuasive interpretations of texts, evaluating how language affects the reader.

4 Rhythm

Learning objective

I am learning:
• to consider the choices poets make about the rhythm and form of their poem.

At GCSE ...

At GCSE you will need to comment on the rhythm and structure of poetry.

Activity 1 Get ready for GCSE

Many poems have a rhythm to them, much like songs. You need to be aware of how poets often deliberately create rhythms to achieve particular effects.

1 Look again at the poem 'I heard a Fly buzz when I died' on page 102.

a Read the poem and think about its rhythm. Notice that there are four heavy beats in the first and third lines. Can you tap this out as you read the first line?

I heard a Fly buzz – when I died –

Was like the Stillness in the Air –

2 How many heavy beats are there in the second line below?

The Stillness in the Room

ResultsPlus
Top tip

Reading a poem aloud can help you work out how the poem is using rhythm to support its meaning.

Activity 2 Get going with GCSE

1 Read Poems 1 and 2 opposite and on page 105. They use a form known as the ballad.

Strictly, a ballad is a form of poetry that alternates between lines of four and three beats, often in groups of 4 lines rhymed *abcb*, and often telling a story. It is also a form that can survive the bending of its rules so sometimes the rhythm and rhyme don't keep to the strict form.

Poem 1

SEA-FEVER By John Masefield

I must down to the seas again, to the lonely sea and the sky,
And all I ask is a tall ship and a star to steer her by,
And the wheel's kick and the wind's song and the white sail's shaking,
And a grey mist on the sea's face and a grey dawn breaking.

5 I must down to the seas again, for the call of the running tide
Is a wild call and a clear call that may not be denied;
And all I ask is a windy day with the white clouds flying,
And the flung spray and the blown spume, and the sea-gulls crying.

I must down to the seas again to the vagrant gypsy life.
10 To the gull's way and the whale's way where the wind's like a whetted knife;
And all I ask is a merry yarn from a laughing fellow-rover,
And quiet sleep and a sweet dream when the long trick's over.

Activity 2 continued...

Poem 2 is written by a modern poet. Look at the background information he provides about this poem, and then read the poem itself.

Poem 2

> I left school when I was fifteen, and when I was fourteen there was this very wonderful teacher who covered his classroom in maps, and he always said when he retired from school, he would go to certain places on these maps. The poem is called 'Geography Lesson'.

Geography Lesson

By Brian Patten

Our teacher told us one day he would leave
And sail across a warm blue sea
To places he had only known from maps,
And all his life had longed to be.

5 The house he lived in was narrow and grey
But in his mind's eye he could see
Sweet-scented jasmine clinging to the walls,
And green leaves burning on an orange tree.

He spoke of the lands he longed to visit,
10 Where it was never drab or cold.
I couldn't understand why he never left,
And shook off the school's stranglehold.

Then halfway through his final term
He took ill and never returned.
15 He never got to that place on the map
Where the green leaves of the orange trees burned.

The maps were redrawn on the classroom wall;
His name forgotten, he faded away.
But a lesson he never knew he taught
20 Is with me to this day.

I travel to where the green leaves burn,
To where the ocean's glass-clear and blue,
To places our teacher taught me to love-
And which he never knew.

Activity 2 continued...

2 Read both poems and look at their titles.

a Masefield's poem shows the power and freedom of the sea and the speaker's desire to be at sea. Look at how this GCSE student has annotated the poem to identify how the rhythm and rhyme help get these ideas across.

> I must down to the seas again, to the lonely sea and the sky,
> And all I ask is a tall ship and a star to steer her by,
> And the wheel's kick and the wind's song and the white sail's shaking,
> And a grey mist on the sea's face and a grey dawn breaking.
>
> I must down to the seas again, for the call of the running tide
> Is a wild call and a clear call that may not be denied;
> And all I ask is a windy day with the white clouds flying,
> And the flung spray and the blown spume, and the sea-gulls crying.
>
> I must down to the seas again to the vagrant gypsy life.
> To the gull's way and the whale's way where the wind's like a whetted knife;
> And all I ask is a merry yarn from a laughing fellow-rover,
> And quiet sleep and a sweet dream when the long trick's over.

> The poet repeats the phrase 'I must' at the start of each stanza. This, along with the rhythm of the poem, emphasises the poet's longing to be at sea again.

> The poet rhymes 'shaking' with 'breaking' and 'flying' with 'crying'. This emphasises the power and energy of the sea.

b What viewpoint do you think Patten's poem conveys?

3 Patten has written two lines where the regular rhythm is disrupted from four to three strong beats.

a Can you find these two lines?

b Why do you think Patten changes the rhythm at these points in the poem? Think about the effect it has on the reader.

4 Look at these statements about the ballad form:

(A) It has lines of four strong beats

(B) It tells a story

(C) Each stanza has four lines (a quatrain)

(D) Lines two and four rhyme (marked as abcb)

(E) There is sometimes a refrain (a repeated line).

a Which of the above features can you find in Poem 1?

b Which of the above features can you find in Poem 2?

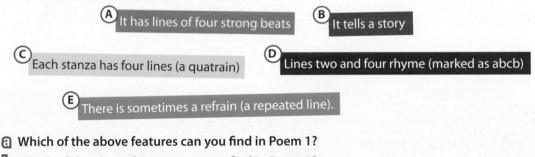

Activity 3 Get ahead at GCSE

1 Patten echoes some of the ideas in the ballad by Masefield.
What similarities and differences can you identify?

a Choose one of the points below. Write one paragraph to compare
the poems on the point you have chosen.
- Mood
- Descriptive language
- Titles
- Final stanza
- Poet's viewpoint

b Try to include information on form, rhythm or rhyme that links to
your point. An example has been done for you.

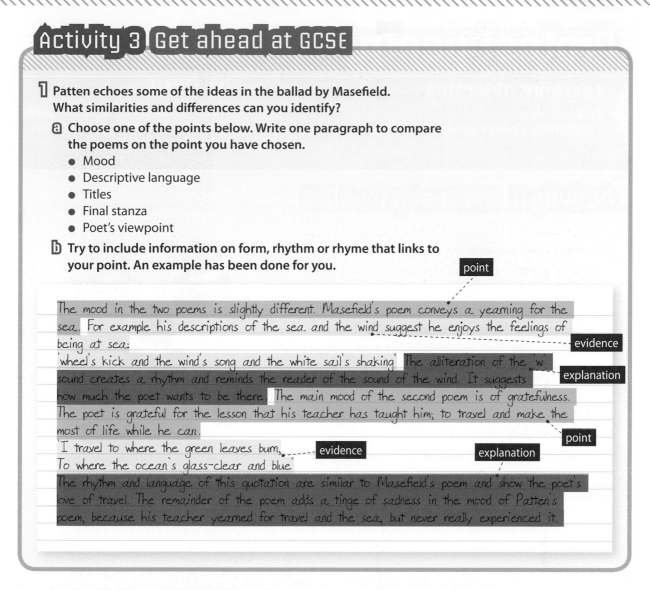

point

The mood in the two poems is slightly different. Masefield's poem conveys a yearning for the
sea. For example his descriptions of the sea and the wind suggest he enjoys the feelings of
being at sea:

evidence

'wheel's kick and the wind's song and the white sail's shaking' The alliteration of the 'w'
sound creates a rhythm and reminds the reader of the sound of the wind. It suggests

explanation

how much the poet wants to be there. The main mood of the second poem is of gratefulness.
The poet is grateful for the lesson that his teacher has taught him; to travel and make the
most of life while he can.

point

'I travel to where the green leaves burn,   evidence   explanation
To where the ocean's glass-clear and blue'

The rhythm and language of this quotation are similar to Masefield's poem and show the poet's
love of travel. The remainder of the poem adds a tinge of sadness in the mood of Patten's
poem, because his teacher yearned for travel and the sea, but never really experienced it.

Assess yourself

Look at your answer to Activity 3. Use the table below to assess your work.

👍 I made general comments about the form, rhythm and rhyme in the poem, using some evidence.	👍👍 I made specific points about the form, rhythm and rhyme in the poem, using evidence from the poem to support my points.	👍👍👍 I carefully explored the form, rhythm and rhyme of the poem, using well-chosen details to support my points.

Now look at the grade descriptions below. They show what you will need to do at GCSE.

Grade F	Grade C	Grade A
Students describe the structure and form of texts, referring to specific details to support their points.	Students understand the effect of the structure and form of texts, referring to specific aspects of language to support their points.	Students evaluate the structure and form of texts, commenting on how they achieve specific effects on the reader.

5 Protest poetry

learning objective

I am learning:
• to identify a poet's viewpoint and concerns.

At GCSE ...

At GCSE you may need to identify the point of view in a poem and analyse how a poet explores it.

Activity 1 Get ready for GCSE

1 Consider the colours in the image opposite.

   a What are their common associations in the UK?

   b Can you think of any common expressions or phrases that use these colours?

   c Choose one colour and create a spider diagram showing common associations like the example below.

Jealousy

Green with envy

New or inexperienced

The grass is always greener

Green

A green light: go!

Going green

Being environmentally friendly

2 Here is a wordbank made from the key words used in the poem you are going to study. Pick out any words that raise a question in your mind. Give reasons for your choice.

> It's interesting that colours often have different associations in different countries. The English superstition is that it's lucky if a black cat crosses your path. In India it is considered unlucky!

art be beaten black book branded by called caught condemned
death don't economy fever guard hailed house joined lies like lived
magic mass master me near people sheep slaved so some spot
suffered trained watch where white whiteleg whitelisted whitemailed
whiteshirts whitesmith whitewater witch wog worry writing

3 Sort as many words as you can into the themes listed in the table below. Add more rows if you can identify any other possible themes.

ResultsPlus
Top tip

A theme is a central idea that runs, like a thread, through a poem, to contribute to its overall meaning.

Theme	Words associated with that theme
Politics	
Freedom	
Colour	
Imprisonment	
Relationships	

Activity 2 Get going with GCSE

1 Now read the poem by Benjamin Zephaniah opposite. It is one of many of his poems that voice protest. There is a long tradition of protest poetry around the world.

2 a How is the poet playing with the words black and white?

b What point do you think he is trying to make?

3 Consider the title of the poem. 'Black comedy' is a phrase generally used in Western society to mean comedy that addresses difficult topics that are generally regarded as taboo. The audience is therefore usually laughing and uncomfortable at the same time. Why do you think the poet chose 'White Comedy' as a title?

4 Consider the final line of the poem. What is the significance of the phrase 'Black House'? What political point do you think Zephaniah is making?

White Comedy

I waz whitemailed
By a white witch,
Wid white magic
An white lies,
5 Branded by a white sheep
I slaved as a whitesmith
Near a white spot
Where I suffered whitewater fever.
Whitelisted as a whiteleg
10 I waz in de white book
As a master of white art,
It waz like white death.

People called me white jack
Some hailed me as a white wog,
15 So I joined de white watch
Trained as a white guard
Lived off the white economy.
Caught and beaten by de whiteshirts
I waz condemned to a white mass,
20 Don't worry,
I shall be writing to de Black House.

Activity 3 Get ahead at GCSE

At GCSE you will need to support the points you make with evidence from the text and explanation, as is the case in the paragraph opposite.

> Zephaniah uses repetition of the word white to highlight how frequently we use insulting terms using the word black. The use of terms beginning with 'white' runs throughout the poem, for example 'whitelisted as a whiteleg'. He also repeats words throughout the poem that can be linked to power and oppression. For example, 'guard...beaten...condemned'. He uses this repetition to suggest that the English language and its common phrases has been too influential and has contributed to a negative view of 'blackness'.

1 Look at the points below. They follow on from the points made in the model paragraph above. Add evidence and explanation to each point.

a Zephaniah uses humour to highlight how insulting and ridiculous these terms are...

b Zephaniah uses shocking language and ideas to make a comment about how English/American language has been the power behind political oppression of black people...

Results Plus
Top tip

Remember to structure each paragraph on poetry using P-E-E: point-evidence-explanation.

6 Comparing poems

learning objective

I am learning:
• to compare two poems.

At GCSE ...

At GCSE you might be asked to compare or write about more than one poem.

ResultsPlus
Top tip

Don't approach poems by spotting poetic terms. You must comment on how they link to the poem's meaning.

Activity 1 Get ready for GCSE

Below are some poetic terms. Match up the terms on the left with their definitions on the right to ensure you have the right vocabulary at your fingertips to respond to poems.

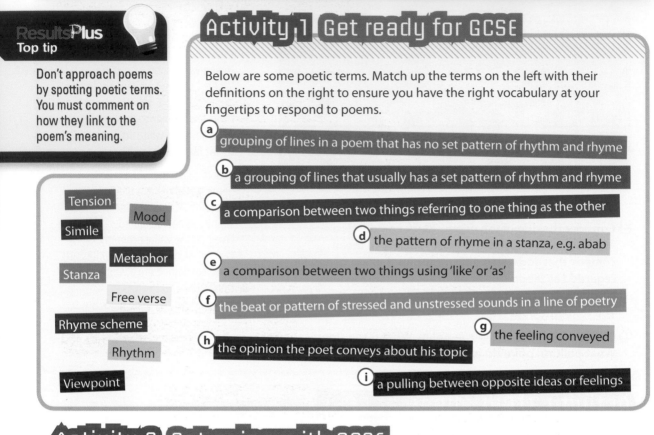

Tension
Mood
Simile
Metaphor
Stanza
Free verse
Rhyme scheme
Rhythm
Viewpoint

(a) grouping of lines in a poem that has no set pattern of rhythm and rhyme

(b) a grouping of lines that usually has a set pattern of rhythm and rhyme

(c) a comparison between two things referring to one thing as the other

(d) the pattern of rhyme in a stanza, e.g. abab

(e) a comparison between two things using 'like' or 'as'

(f) the beat or pattern of stressed and unstressed sounds in a line of poetry

(g) the feeling conveyed

(h) the opinion the poet conveys about his topic

(i) a pulling between opposite ideas or feelings

Activity 2 Get going with GCSE

1 Remind yourself of the poem on page 96 called 'Illuminations'. Select a quotation from the poem to support each of the points opposite.

2 Identify one feature of the poem you found interesting and complete the sentence below.

I found this poem interesting because ...

Topic: the poem is about a childhood holiday in Blackpool. The speaker/poet remembers a disagreement with his father, but now as an adult understands his father better.

Mood: the mood changes from excitement at the beginning, through anger in the middle to sadness at the end as he remembers his father.

Form/Structure: The poem is written in 3 stanzas which reflect the poet's changing mood from past to present. The poet also uses italic text to reflect his father's speech.

Viewpoint: The poet feels sad about the loss of his father and understands him better now he is an adult.

Language: The poet links the idea of understanding and the holiday destination of Blackpool through the word 'Illuminations'. He also uses words connected with the amusements there.

Activity 3 Get ahead at GCSE

Now read a second poem about a family holiday by Choman Hardi, from Iraqi Kurdistan, together with the annotations below. Think about what is similar and different in relation to 'Illuminations'.

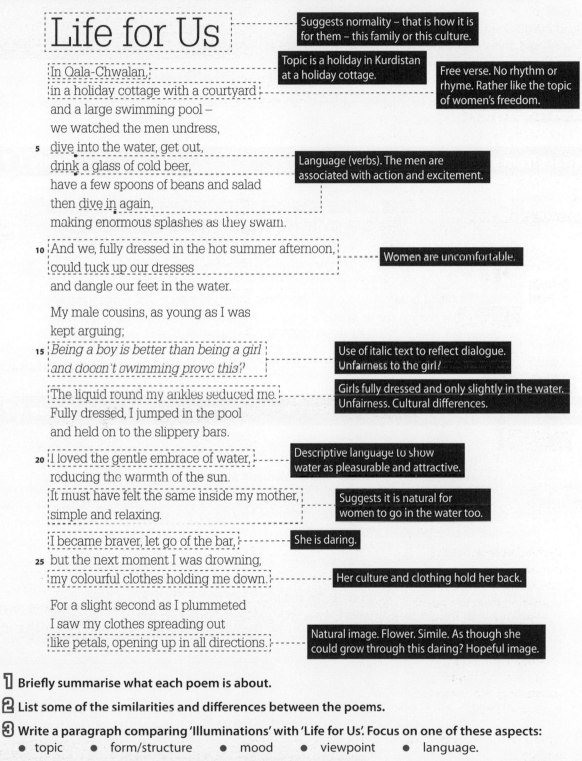

Life for Us

> Suggests normality – that is how it is for them – this family or this culture.

In Qala-Chwalan,
in a holiday cottage with a courtyard
and a large swimming pool –
we watched the men undress,

> Topic is a holiday in Kurdistan at a holiday cottage.

> Free verse. No rhythm or rhyme. Rather like the topic of women's freedom.

5   dive into the water, get out,
drink a glass of cold beer,
have a few spoons of beans and salad
then dive in again,
making enormous splashes as they swam.

> Language (verbs). The men are associated with action and excitement.

10 And we, fully dressed in the hot summer afternoon,
could tuck up our dresses
and dangle our feet in the water.

> Women are uncomfortable.

My male cousins, as young as I was
kept arguing;
15 *Being a boy is better than being a girl*
and doesn't swimming prove this?

> Use of italic text to reflect dialogue. Unfairness to the girl?

The liquid round my ankles seduced me.
Fully dressed, I jumped in the pool
and held on to the slippery bars.

> Girls fully dressed and only slightly in the water. Unfairness. Cultural differences.

20 I loved the gentle embrace of water,
reducing the warmth of the sun.
It must have felt the same inside my mother,
simple and relaxing.

> Descriptive language to show water as pleasurable and attractive.

> Suggests it is natural for women to go in the water too.

I became braver, let go of the bar,

> She is daring.

25 but the next moment I was drowning,
my colourful clothes holding me down.

> Her culture and clothing hold her back.

For a slight second as I plummeted
I saw my clothes spreading out
like petals, opening up in all directions.

> Natural image. Flower. Simile. As though she could grow through this daring? Hopeful image.

1 Briefly summarise what each poem is about.

2 List some of the similarities and differences between the poems.

3 Write a paragraph comparing 'Illuminations' with 'Life for Us'. Focus on one of these aspects:
- topic
- form/structure
- mood
- viewpoint
- language

In this activity you are going to look at some extracts from sample answers to Activity 3 on page 111. An examiner has commented on the extracts and suggested a grade, but he has not shown which comment belongs to which extract.

Your task:
- Read the different student answer extracts.
- As you read, think about the strengths and weaknesses of the answers
- Read the examiner's comments.
- Work out which comment belongs to which answer.

Like a real examiner, you could be asked to explain your choices so make sure you have reasons ready to support your answers.

Extract from student answer 1	Grade

'Illuminations' and 'Life for us' look back at the poets' childhoods and remember the mood at that moment. Harrison's poem shows two different moods. His father is angry and frustrated because his son wants to play on the machines. The son is excited and then he is angry.

'I sulked all week'

At the end the mood is sad. 'Life for Us' also shows different moods. The poet remembers feeling angry that she cannot do what the boys do. It shows that rules for men and women in her society are unfair. She feels happy when she does what she wants and goes in the water. 'I loved the gentle embrace of water.'

Extract from student answer 2	Grade

'Illuminations' and 'Life for Us' have very different moods. The first poem moves between three different moods to show the poet's childhood and then his mood as an adult. It moves from excitement to anger to sadness. The mood at the end of the poem is sad as the poet understands why his father acted like that. He misses him. 'Wish you were here.' This is a phrase that is used on postcards because he is remembering a holiday, but now probably his father is dead.

In 'Life for Us' the main mood of the poem is frustration as the girl is being teased and cannot do what she wants. The mood at the end might be hopeful. The opening flower might symbolise that the girl took a risk but she is free and doing something natural, 'Like petals'.

Extract from student answer 3   Grade

'Illuminations' and 'Life for Us' are similar in their mood. Adults are looking back to the past. They are feeling emotional about when they were little. Harrison shows that he misses his father. Hardi shows that she was angry with her brothers and thought it was unfair. The boy enjoyed the fair as lots of children like us enjoy amusements. He is excited. There were a lot of games to go on and the boy can't stop thinking about them. He wants to go on them all the time. It's like he is obsessed.

(E) Examiner comment 1

This extract from the student's answer is typical of E grade performance. The student makes a simple response to the poem. The response makes just one main point of comparison, focusing on the mood of the poems. While the student does show knowledge and understanding of the poem, they do not select or use any evidence to support the points they makes. The response includes some irrelevant material where the candidate loses focus on the question. If the student sustained this level throughout their response, it is likely that they would achieve a grade E.

(D) Examiner comment 2

This extract from the student's answer is typical of D grade performance. The student identifies a range of points about the mood of the two poems and includes evidence from the poem to support these points. If the student sustained this level in the rest of their response, they would most likely achieve a grade D. The student could have improved the answer by going on to explain the effect of the evidence selected.

(C) Examiner comment 3

This extract from the student's answer is typical of C grade performance. The response accurately identifies the range of different moods in the two poems and there is some good use of evidence to support the points the student is making. The student also identifies a poetic technique – the use of the flower as a symbol – and explains its meaning, although there is still scope for the student to explore the 'like petals' simile further. If the student sustained this type of writing throughout their response, they would probably achieve a grade C.

---

1 Now look back at your answer to this activity. Compare it to the three extracts from student answers on these pages.
   • Which one is your answer closest to?
   • Discuss or jot down what you might need to do to improve your answer if you were
     to do it again.

7 Tackling unseen poems in the future

learning objective

I am learning:
- about strategies for approaching poems I have not read before.

At GCSE ...

At GCSE you will need to read and respond to poems you have not seen before.

Over the course of this unit you have learnt a number of ways in which you can tackle poems that you have not read before. You can use some or all of these approaches in the future, and at GCSE, when responding to unseen poems.

Step 1: What is the poem about?

The first question you might want to ask about a poem is: what is it about? Poems are carefully constructed and need careful reading. As a reader, you need to investigate the poem to pinpoint its meanings. Look at the spider diagram below which shows some of the ways in which you might do this.

A person, an event, a place, an idea, a feeling? Or something else?

What does the title suggest the poem will be about? What does the title make you think of?

Does the first line reveal what the poem is about?

What is the poem about?

Do the words the poet has chosen to use suggest anything about the poem's meaning?

Does the last line reveal any more about the poem's meaning?

Who is the speaker in the poem?

Step 2: What is the poet trying to do?

Once you've gained an initial impression of what the poem is about, next you could explore the key ideas and meanings the poet is trying to get across. Look at some of the questions you might ask yourself.

What is the speaker's point of view?

How is the speaker feeling?

What is the mood of the poem - happy, sad, threatening, peaceful? Something else?

What are the key ideas or meanings in the poem?

How does the poem make you feel?

Step 3: finding details from the poem

Now that you've thought about what the poem is about and its key ideas and meanings, the next step could be to find important details from the poem. Approach the poem like a detective to identify the clues to meaning – in this case, details from the poem. You could look for:

As you read the poem, annotate any significant details you can identify.

- Particular words or phrases the poet has used that really make an impression or have a clear impact on the reader.
- Language techniques the poet has used such as alliteration, imagery, repetition, and so on.

Step 4: Thinking about structure and form

The effect of a poem isn't just down to the words the poet has used. The structure and form of a poem can also add to its meaning and impact. The poet has made a deliberate choice about the structure and form to write in. Look at the spider diagram below to help you get started when thinking about the structure and form of a poem.

Does it rhyme the whole way through? If it changes at all, is this deliberate?

What is the rhyme scheme?

Is it organised into stanzas? If so, are all the stanzas the same length? If the stanzas are of different lengths, is this deliberate?

Does the poem rhyme?

Structure and form

What is the effect of any rhymes or half rhymes? For example, do they emphasise certain words or ideas?

How is the poem organised?

If the poem is arranged into stanzas, does the poet explore different ideas in the stanzas? Or do things like the mood, tense or speaker change across the stanzas?

Does the poet vary the length of the lines in the poem? If so, what is the effect of this?

Step 5: Putting it all together

Finally, put all of the above steps together to help you write your response to the poem. Your exact response will depend upon the question you are being asked to answer, but in general you should show you know:

- What the poem is about.
- What the poet is trying to achieve or say in the poem.
- How you think the poet achieves this through use of language, literary devices and structure.

Activity Get going with GCSE

Try putting this strategy into practice now.

1. **Find a poem you haven't read before.**

2. **Go through steps 1 to 5 above.**

3. **Write your response to the poem, saying what you think it is about and how effective the poem is – a bit like a book review. Keep it simple at first – you could focus on a particular stanza or section of the poem.**

ResultsPlus
Top tip

Try to practise tackling unknown poems on a regular basis – the more you do it, the more skilled you will become.

8 Getting personal

learning objective

I am learning:
- to plan and write a piece of personal writing using the first person.

At GCSE ...

At GCSE you may need to structure a piece of personal writing to interest your reader.

Activity 1 Get ready for GCSE

Read the opening paragraphs below from two pieces of personal writing about regret.

1 **Make some notes to compare the texts. You could think about:**

- use of first person/third person (use of I/she, he or it)
- information about **w**ho, **w**hat, **w**hen and **w**here the event(s) took place
- use of time indicators to structure the writing (e.g. finally, next, last week, in the morning)
- use of language to indicate the writer's feelings
- how the writer makes the reader want to read on.

Extract A

I threw £100000 in the bin

That February morning was just like any other. I parked my Royal Mail van by the newsagent's, made my delivery and nipped to the counter for tobacco and scratchcards. It was a habit I'd fallen into – money had been tight for months. With three children to support, my wife and I frequently argued, so these cards offered the tantalising possibility of an easier life.

Extract B

I served 25 years for a crime I didn't commit

For me, 13 November is a memorable day. It took less than an hour for the Court of Appeal to overturn my conviction for murder and I was finally allowed to walk free after serving 25 years for a crime I didn't commit.

I went to prison in 1977 – the year of the Queen's silver jubilee and when the Bay City Rollers were still getting number ones and I was 19. I'd moved to Manchester from Glasgow, where I'd grown up, to start a new life and escape the cycle of poverty and crime I had drifted into.

2 **Notice that Extract A tells the story from the beginning. It is written in chronological order. Extract B begins at the end and then moves to the beginning in paragraph 2. Why do you think the author of Extract B does this?**

Look at how the author of Extract B goes on to show how he felt.

'I walked from the Court of Appeal with my shoulders hunched and my eyes downcast'

The author could have just written:

'I was crushed and emotionally damaged by being sent to prison'

Activity 1 continued...

Good writing **shows** rather than **tells** the reader. The first line shows he felt crushed and emotionally damaged. The second just tells us that.

❸ Think of a line to add to Extract A to suggest that as he approached the counter for his scratchcard he was full of desperate hope.

Results Plus
Top tip

Show don't tell! Convey your emotions by your choice of language rather than stating how you felt. For example, it's more effective to say 'I ran from the house at full pelt, not daring to look back' rather than 'I felt really scared'.

Activity 2 Get going with GCSE

At GCSE, you need to spend time thinking about what you are going to write before you start writing. The best writing will have been carefully planned.

❶ Look at the question below.

> Write about an event that you regret.

ⓐ Jot down some ideas that you might use from your own life. They will probably be less sensational than the extracts on the previous page! Make sure you write down at least 3 ideas.

ⓑ Now reconsider your ideas. Use the checklist opposite to decide on the final idea to use in your personal writing. A good choice will mean you can answer 'yes' to most of the questions.

❷ Now write out the title of your personal writing about regret. Sketch out a timeline with 5 key elements that you could use to structure your writing.

	YES	NO
Did the event actually happen to you?	☐	☐
Can you clearly identify one or two emotions that you felt during the event?	☐	☐
Can you describe the setting?	☐	☐
Can you picture the scene?	☐	☐
Can you remember details about what happened?	☐	☐
Can you think of a moment where the event began and a moment where it ended?	☐	☐
Did you learn anything from the event?	☐	☐
Is your topic appropriate to share with other readers?	☐	☐

Activity 3 Get ahead at GCSE

❶ Now write the opening paragraph of your piece. Like Extracts A and B on page 116, you need to:
- use the first person
- establish factual information to support your reader (who, what, when, where)
- consider beginning with the first or last point in time
- convey your emotions about the event through your choice of language.

At GCSE many students lose marks because they do not check their work for accurate spelling and punctuation.

❷ Check what you have written. Take care that spelling and punctuation are accurate.

9 Striking sentences

Learning objective

I am learning:
• to vary my sentence length and vocabulary for effect.

At GCSE …

At GCSE the examiners will look at whether you use vocabulary and sentence structures deliberately to create particular effects in your creative writing.

Activity 1 Get ready for GCSE

1 Read the text opposite from an adult science fiction book.

a Identify any words and phrases that the publisher uses to encourage a reader to want to buy the book.

b Can you find examples of:
- minor sentences (very short sentences, sometimes just one or two words)
- short sentences
- long sentences
- ellipses (…)?

2 Now choose two of the sections you have identified and write a point-evidence-explanation paragraph explaining the effect of what the writer has done. An example has been done for you below.

> The writer uses short clipped sentences in the blurb. For example the minor sentence 'And beyond' is used '. This is used to create a feeling of suspense and encourage a reader to buy the book to find out more

ResultsPlus
Top tip

Good writers use short and long sentences with purpose. Each can be used to reflect a particular mood, create rhythm and deliberately affect the reader.

> 'What strange places our lives can carry us to.
>
> What dark passages…'
>
> Deep in the jungles of eastern Colombia, Professor Jonas Lear has finally found what he's been searching for – and wishes to God he hadn't.
>
> Bound together in ways they cannot comprehend, for each of them a door is about to open into a future they could not have imagined. And a journey is about to begin. An epic journey that will take them through a world transformed by man's darkest dreams, to the very heart of what it means to be human.
>
> And beyond.

Activity 2 Get going with GCSE

1 Read Tony Harrrison's poem on Blackpool on page 96 again. Look at the picture opposite, and the one on page 96 to remind you of the atmosphere and rides at a funfair. Then look at the question below.

Describe a fairground.

- Use your choice of language and sentence structures to convey a threatening mood.
- You might describe a threatening scenario – for example, someone is lost, someone has run away or a fairground ride is going to collapse.

Activity 2 continued...

2 Create a wordbank of interesting words and phrases that will help describe the scene, using a table like the one below.

Nouns that establish the topic of the fairground	Words and phrases that link to the senses
Carousel Ghost train Candy floss	The buzz of the generators The clatter of the ghost train

3 Now write up to three paragraphs of a descriptive piece to convey the atmosphere and mood of the fairground. Remember that to impress a GCSE examiner you will need to use:
- a range of interesting vocabulary, spelled correctly
- a variety of sentence lengths used for effect.

ResultsPlus
Watch out!

On page 117 you wrote in the first person (I). For this piece, use the third person (he/she/it). Check your work to ensure you maintain this throughout your written piece.

Activity 3 Get ahead at GCSE

You can learn how to improve your own creative writing by looking at how the professionals do it!

1 Read this passage from a detective novel by Susan Hill. It describes a funfair in a town where a gunman has been on the rampage. The police and the public are tense...

Find:
- an example of a short sentence used to create tension
- an example of a long sentence used for effect
- examples of interesting, descriptive vocabulary that convey the scene of the fair.

2 Now have a look at the writing you did in Activity 2.
a Are there any improvements you could make?
b Check you have a range of examples of different sentence structures and vocabulary for effect.

1 Helen exploded with laughter and let Phil pull her by the hand towards the candyfloss stall. The smell of burnt sugar mingled with the diesel fumes of the generators and the burning oil from the burger stalls on the smoky night air. It was eight o'clock and the Jug Fair was packed. Helen looked up at the Sky-Dyve plunging giddily down and at the sparks and crackles from the bumper cars and felt like one of the kids.

2 The candyfloss queue snaked round and back and mingled with the queue for hot dogs and another for toffee apples.

3 'God, this is fun. I haven't been since Tom and Lizzie were in single figures.'

4 'Place is knee-deep in cops.'

5 'Not surprised. This is just the sort of event where a gunman could run amok. Look around...all those points a sniper could stand.'

6 Helen's eyes were drawn to the Sky-Dyve. If a man...at the top of the helter skelter. If...

7 A gun cracked loudly not far away.

8 Phil put a reassuring hand on her arm. 'Shooting ducks.'

10 Purpose and audience

learning objective
I am learning:
• to write creatively for a specific purpose and audience.

At GCSE ...
At GCSE, to write successfully means being able to understand what you are writing and who you are writing it for.

Activity 1 Get ready for GCSE

1 A script is the written form of a spoken text. Read the transcript from a Newsround television item about 'The Frozen Ark'.

Extinct animals could be brought to life

Newsreader: Loads of you will know the biblical story of the Ark. Noah took two of every animal and packed them on board to save them from a giant flood.

In the story it worked: they survived and had babies, who had babies, who had babies [fading echo] And the animal kingdom lived on.

[cut to shot of scientist in laboratory]

And this is the modern day Ark. Instead of whole animals this place stores tiny amounts of their blood frozen to protect it from damage. The blood contains DNA. Every animal's DNA is different and it contains the instructions for creating life. If an animal does die out, scientists hope in the future they'll be able to use its DNA to bring it back.

Scientist 1: There is a very real possibility we might be able to bring back an extinct or a very endangered species. And that can't be anything but good.

Newsreader: And this is one of those endangered animals: the Sun bear is the world's smallest type of bear – cute but very fierce. Today vets are taking a small sample of its blood to send to The Frozen Ark. They're trying to get blood from as many animals as possible before it's too late.

Scientist 2: We're just not saving some of these species in the wild or even in zoos, we just, we can't do it, we haven't got the resources, we're losing them too quickly.

Newsreader: There are no guarantees the Frozen Ark will bring back animals like these if they do die out and some people think it's wrong to try and create life artificially. Some scientists say the Ark could be their only hope.

The audience for this news transcript is young people. The purpose is to inform and entertain.

2 The features below are typical of good information writing for young people. Can you find any examples of them in the transcript?
● Informal language
● Contractions ('they're' rather than 'they are')
● Facts
● Familiar references
● Short sentences
● Simple vocabulary
● Explanations of technical terms or difficult words
● Quotations from experts

Activity 2 Get going with GCSE

Scientists are trying to bring the woolly mammoth back to life by using its frozen DNA to fertilise elephant eggs.

1 Can you name any extinct creatures?

2 You are going to write a fictional news report for children's television about resurrecting an extinct creature. To prepare for your writing:

- choose one animal you are interested in and find a picture of it
- find out as many facts as you can about that animal to prepare for your writing. You might use books, magazines or the Internet to do this
- alternatively, you could make up a creature and make up the 'facts' about that creature
- decide which of this information you might include in a news report for young people; discard any which is too complex for that audience.

Activity 3 Get ahead at GCSE

1 Now write the script for your news item. Include facts and scientific information to inform your teenage audience. Write in a style that reflects the *Newsround* text you studied on page 120.

2 If you have time, perform your news report in front of a partner.

Assess yourself

Look at the transcript you wrote in Activity 3. Use the table below to assess your work.

👍 I made some effort to match my writing to the purpose and audience.	👍👍 I clearly identified and focused my writing on the purpose and audience.	👍👍👍 I made sure the content, language and style of my writing was matched to the purpose and audience.

Now look at the grade descriptions below. They show what you will need to do at GCSE.

Grade **F**	Grade **C**	Grade **A**
Students show some ability to match the form and style of their writing for different tasks and purposes.	Students can successfully adapt the form and style of their writing for different tasks and purposes.	Students have a confident grasp of a range of forms and styles and can match these to different tasks and purposes.

11 Form and genre

learning objective

I am learning:
- to consider forms of writing and how to change a text from one form to another.

At GCSE ...

At GCSE you could write in the form of a monologue.

Activity 1 Get ready for GCSE

The poem opposite is by Simon Armitage. It is in the form of a monologue, which is a spoken poem from one person's viewpoint.

Read the poem then answer the questions below about what it tells us.

1 List the people that the boy knows. How do you think he knows them?

2 What does he like about the fire station?

3 What does the last stanza tell us about what this boy does?

4 List three things that the man in the post office thinks about the boy.

5 In what way might the boy be a criminal?

6 Do you feel any sympathy or understanding for the boy and why? Underline any words or phrases that help you understand this boy.

7 Think about the poem's title. Why do you think that Armitage doesn't give the boy a name?

The Boy Outside the Fire Station
By Simon Armitage

Anyway, I'm mad. I know this as a fact
Because him in the Post Office said I was.
He tried to tell Joey when he cashed his Giro
And he knows damn well I'm not deaf.

I just like watching. Have you seen how clean it is?
Clean as a kitchen. Cleaner. I had a good look
Last week before they closed them concertina doors.
Cleaner than the bloody Post Office anyway.

And I like how they're always half dressed.
It's like a scrum in that cabin when they set off,
Buttoning their flies up or getting into their boots right.
Anne says they argue about ringing the bell.

Digger, he's only a part-time volunteer, says
He's only ever missed a call-out once
When he was getting to the pitch with his missis.
He reckons they'll get them bleeper things in next year.

I'm always ready, watching when the siren goes
And they pile out of their houses in pyjamas,
Pulling them blue jerseys over their heads
And wobbling down Manchester Road on their bikes.

Him at the Post Office knows I'm up to something.
Well, I stink of petrol, and he's seen my matches
And he knows damn well I don't smoke.
But he's frightened to death of saying anything.

Activity 2 Get going with GCSE

Now let's create an explosion chart of all the possible stories that could branch out form this poem.

1 Look at the linear structure of the poem, shown below. Can you add any boxes to the explosion chart to map out extra possibilities for writing linked to the last two points?

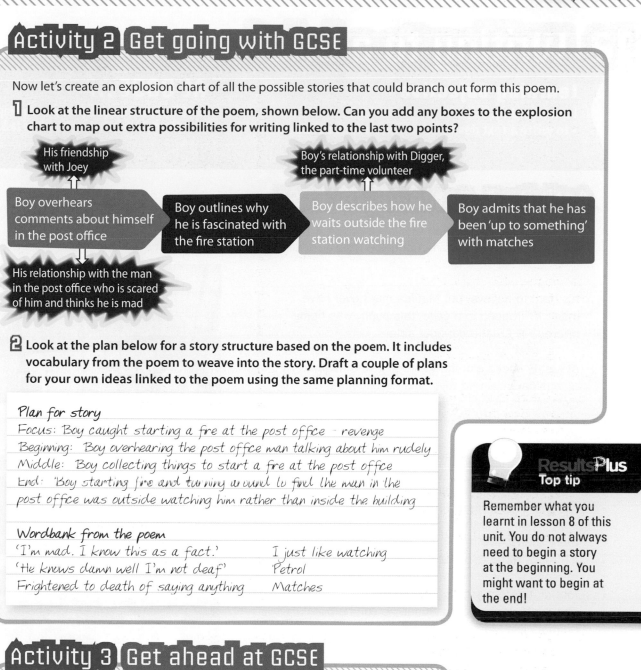

His friendship with Joey

Boy's relationship with Digger, the part-time volunteer

Boy overhears comments about himself in the post office → Boy outlines why he is fascinated with the fire station → Boy describes how he waits outside the fire station watching → Boy admits that he has been 'up to something' with matches

His relationship with the man in the post office who is scared of him and thinks he is mad

2 Look at the plan below for a story structure based on the poem. It includes vocabulary from the poem to weave into the story. Draft a couple of plans for your own ideas linked to the poem using the same planning format.

Plan for story
Focus: Boy caught starting a fire at the post office - revenge
Beginning: Boy overhearing the post office man talking about him rudely
Middle: Boy collecting things to start a fire at the post office
End: Boy starting fire and turning around to find the man in the post office was outside watching him rather than inside the building

Wordbank from the poem

'I'm mad. I know this as a fact.'	I just like watching
'He knows damn well I'm not deaf'	Petrol
Frightened to death of saying anything	Matches

Results Plus
Top tip

Remember what you learnt in lesson 8 of this unit. You do not always need to begin a story at the beginning. You might want to begin at the end!

Activity 3 Get ahead at GCSE

1 Now choose one of the plans and begin writing your story. Remember what you have learnt so far about good writing:

- Choose the first or third person and maintain it throughout.
- Choose interesting vocabulary and sentence structures to interest the reader.
- Think about what the reader will be able to see, smell, hear, etc. when reading your writing. How will you appeal to the senses?

2 Now proofread your work for spelling and punctuation errors.

Results Plus
Top tip

You may want to include some dialogue in your story. Make sure that your story also includes plot and description as well as sections of dialogue.

12 Writing to a brief

learning objective

I am learning:
• to write a text designed to persuade the reader.

At GCSE ...

At GCSE you will need to show you can adapt your writing to suit the purpose of the task.

Activity 1 Get ready for GCSE

Look at the images and transcript below from an advert from the animal charity The Blue Cross.

1 It's hard to believe, but Matilda may never have made it. Trapped in a cage, this puppy was being offered for £5 at a car boot sale.

2 At just 8 weeks old she was being sold as junk alongside unwanted toys, and second-hand clothes. Thankfully a horrified animal lover paid for her and brought her to us so she could get a second chance in life.

3 At The Blue Cross we take in abandoned, neglected and unwanted animals. We give them food, love, veterinary care and behavioural support and find them new homes. It costs us more than £450 to raise a needy puppy until it's ready to be re-homed. And that's one of the reasons why we need your support. There are lots of different ways to give to The Blue Cross. Thanks to your kind donations we can help animals like Matilda again and again.

1 What is the text type, audience and purpose of this text?

2 Can you identify examples of factual information from the text?

3 How do the images support this?

4 a Can you identify examples of persuasive rhetorical devices in this text?
For example:
● repetition
● use of the second person 'you'
● emotive language.

b How do the images add to the text's persuasiveness?

Activity 2 Get going with GCSE

Look at the cat below, together with a letter from his previous owner to The Blue Cross.

> Dear Blue Cross,
>
> Thank you for helping me to find a new home for Tiger. After the birth of our new baby I am finding him too tricky. I am worried that he might sit on or scratch the baby. He likes to hunt, and I am having to clear up all kinds of debris from mice entrails to pigeon feathers on a daily basis. My partner has now said there is no way she will live with him any more.
>
> Yours, Angus

1 What could potential owners find attractive about this cat's appearance and personality?

2 What might be the drawbacks of having him as a pet?

3 Can you identify how these drawbacks could be viewed in a positive way? What kind of household might he suit?

Activity 3 Get ahead at GCSE

1 Imagine you work for The Blue Cross charity. Your job is to write the online video advert to appeal for someone to volunteer to re-home Tiger. It needs to:
- be factual and persuasive
- give Tiger the best possible chance of a new owner
- ensure potential owners understand what they are taking on.

a Use the template like the one below to write a storyboard for an advert for Tiger.

b You need to give information for at least 5 images you will use and write the persuasive and informative text for the advert.

IMAGE 1 [insert description of image here]	IMAGE 2 [insert description of image here]	IMAGE 3 [insert description of image here]
Text to accompany IMAGE 1	Text to accompany IMAGE 2	Text to accompany IMAGE 3

In this activity you are going to look at extracts from some sample answers to Activity 3 on page 117. Remind yourself of the task below:

> Write about an event that you regret.

Re-cap everything you have learnt in this unit. A skilled writer considers:

- planning
- a sense of place (who, what, when, where)
- description that appeals to the senses
- showing not telling
- an awareness of beginning, middle, end
- a conscious choice of where, in time, to begin the story
- a range of sentence structures and punctuation
- accurate punctuation and spelling.

1a The extracts from student responses below contain a mixture of strengths and weaknesses. Read each one and choose five places where you would give praise ✓. Where would you place the ticks and why?

b Then choose five places where the students could improve their answers, and give some reasons.

Extract from student answer 1   Grade ?

Did u ever read that story in primary school about the little boy who stole someone else's balaclarva and then was totally scared about what he had done? Its like what happened to me! The day that I ate the chocolates from Mr Webster's sports bag was what I always regretted! For one thing, he is nice! And secondly, even worse, I got caught! You know what they say it's alright as long as you get away with it.

Extract from student answer 2   Grade ?

24th December is a day I will always remember. My granddad died and I didn't see him.

That morning my mum got a phone call. 'Grandad's ill,' she said. 'Do you want to come with me? Her words whirling round my head. I was half asleep. Grandad and I had never jelled. I was wrecked from the end of term. The thought of having to spend the morning in my grandads' boiling hot smelly tiny flat with a few rich tea biscuits wasnt all that. My bed or going out in a December morning. I chose what most teenagers would like. I stayed in bed. I felt a bit gilty about it afterwards, maybe I should have gone and supported everyone but at the time it felt like the right thing to do.

'If you swear really loudly in front of your mum when she comes to pick you up from school, I will give you that Lego man,' I promised Bertie. In fact, I will give you two.' He looked at me with his eyes wide and nodded. We were in year 5 and we were obsessed with swapping and increasing our Lego collections. I had decided it was about time his mum stopped thinking he was totally brilliant and realised he was just an ordinary kid like us. It might have been the day that Bertie got himself into trouble, but I got myself into deeper trouble than ever, with Mr Marlowe the headteacher and...even more scarily... with my own mum!

2 Now rank the extracts, with the best first. Give reasons for your choices.

3 Re-read the extract that you ranked as number 3. Read the examiner's comments below. Which of them would you link to this piece of writing?

> Uses Standard English   Spells most words accurately   Punctuation is generally accurate

> Uses a variety of punctuation   Uses a variety of sentence structures including complex sentences

> Uses interesting description to convey mood and place

> Writing is appropriately formal   Some attempt to interest the reader

4 Write down three suggestions of how to improve the piece you ranked as number 3.

5 Now look at your own answer to this activity. Compare it to the three student extracts on these pages.
  a Which one is your answer closest to?
  b Discuss or jot down what you might need to do to improve your answer if you were to do it again.

6 Write an advice sheet for students tackling this kind of question at GCSE. In your advice sheet include what they should do (for example, they should always check their work at the end) and what they should not do (for example, they should not just ignore the specified audience and purpose of the task).